Unamuno's Paratexts

Juan de la Cuesta
Hispanic Monographs

FOUNDING EDITOR
Tom Lathrop
University of Delaware

EDITOR
Alexander R. Selimov
University of Delaware

EDITORIAL BOARD
Samuel G. Armistead
University of California, Davis

Annette G. Cash
Georgia State University

Alan Deyermond
Queen Mary and Westfield College of the University of London

Daniel Eisenberg
Excelsior College

John E. Keller
University of Kentucky

Steven D. Kirby
Eastern Michigan University

Joel Rini
University of Virginia

Donna M. Rogers
Middlebury College

Russell P. Sebold
University of Pennsylvania, Emeritus
Corresponding Member, Real Academia Española

Noël Valis
Yale University

Amy Williamsen
University of Arizona

Unamuno's Paratexts: Twisted Guides to Contorted Narratives

by

THOMAS R. FRANZ
Ohio University

Juan de la Cuesta
Newark, Delaware

Copyright © 2006 by Juan de la Cuesta—Hispanic Monographs
270 Indian Road
Newark, Delaware 19711
(302) 453-8695
Fax: (302) 453-8601
www.JuandelaCuesta.com

MANUFACTURED IN THE UNITED STATES OF AMERICA

ISBN: 1-58871-094-7

To the memory of my parents,
RUDY and MARY ANN FRANZ

Contents

Introduction 9

Principal Paratexts of Unamuno's Narratives 21

Texts and Paratexts in the Unamunian Style 27

Dedications and Epigraphs 37

Introductions, Prologues, Prefaces 47

Notes 81

Epilogues 89

Epitexts 99

Conclusions 111

Works Cited 121

Introduction

ALMOST AS MUCH AS the thematic concerns of life after death (Marías 50) and the human personality (Blanco Aguinaga 31), the novelistic fiction of Unamuno is characterized by its paratexts. Open almost any of his longer narratives or collections thereof, and one will find preludes to or extensions of their central text: epigraphs, prologues of various sorts, disguised and undisguised epilogues, notes, and—for the reader familiar with his endless collections of other kinds of writing—an inexhaustible supply of epitexts. This paratextual presence, so obvious, so seemingly distinct from the presumed narrative core of the work, must—one suspects—play an integral role in the narrative's dramatization of the quest for immortality and the unfolding of the mechanisms of personality. In a novelist whose work is highly formalistic—this despite its author's coinage of terms like *vivíparo* and *nivola* and the critic's habitual application of descriptors like "open" or "unclosured"—one easily perceives that the form of the work, and hence its overall message or the experience of its reader, depends on that reader's attention to those elements given inordinate emphasis by being set off from the central text.

In 1987, Genette published *Seuils*, the bible of paratextual vademecums. Ten years later it became available in English as *Paratexts: Thresholds of Interpretation*. Some variation ultimately exists between the original French, the English translation, and terms used by Unamuno. Genette speaks of the *préface* in reference to phenomena that English would subsume under either *preface* or *prologue*. Although *prefacio* exists in Spanish, Unamuno invariably prefers *prólogo*, whether referring to a prologue or a preface. These variations make little difference provided the translator or critic add clarifiers to make more precise any use of the terms. In this study, many words—*prologue, preface, prelude,* and *introduction*—are adapted as counterparts to Genette's *préface*. Some of this is done for stylistic variation, but most is carried out in an attempt to modulate Genette's highly flexible use of an otherwise inflexible lexicon for its current employment in a study written in English. There are, for example, many places in which the English-language reader of the rigidly translated *preface* (for *préface*) would understand an appendage written by a real or imagined third party, when Genette more often refers clearly to a text added by the author or one of his or her characters. In instances such as this, some flexibility in the rendering of terminology is necessary if one is to both keep up with Genette's multiple denotations and provide descriptions of forms utilized by Unamuno.

I am obviously not the only commentator on Unamuno's fiction to discuss Unamuno's paratexts, but the present study is, at writing, the only one to focus on the entire body of his extended fiction. Almost no study of specific Unamuno narratives is without some reference and speculation as to the function of one or more of its paratexts. This is particularly true in almost every study dealing with *Amor y pedagogía* (1902) and *Niebla* (1914). A very few studies of Unamuno's narrative art have foregrounded the phenomenon of paratextual structures. Criado's 1986 work, *Las novelas de Unamuno: estudio formal y crítico,* makes liberal use of Genette's perspectives, but the French theorist's material appears here imbedded in formalist concerns of a larger order—the overall structuring of plot and characterization—so that it becomes diluted, at times even distorted, in observations on discourse and diegesis quite alien to Genette's more limited claims for paratextual analysis. Vauthier's 1999 study, *Niebla de Miguel de Unamuno: A favor de Cervantes, en contra de los "cervantófilos,"* on the other hand, while severely limited to one novel, faithfully and creatively uses Genette's paratextual catalogue and its illustrative exposition of effects in order to tease important metaliterary—though few ontological—perspectives from Unamuno's most famous narratives. Pérez López applauds the achievements of Vauthier and categorically states that it is the paratextual elements that free Unamuno's narratives from the dictates of positivism and the quasi-deterministic structures of realism (69-79). I have attempted to combine Criado's highly justified attention to diegesis with Vauthier's more concentrated attention to the paratexts. I have added to these concerns an attempt to define the effects of this paratextual-diegetical link to Unamuno's problematic ontology, a personal interest of mine that it is fair to say is common to many Unamuno commentators of my own and earlier generations.

It will be observed—perhaps with some surprise—that my view of the paratexts' contribution to the creation of a narrative ontology is an optimistic one. That is, my martialing of evidence leads to an unmistakable conclusion that the paratexual material in Unamuno's narratives counteracts and successfully reverses much of the pessimistic and "tragic" dimension created by the narratives' central texts. My reaction to this conclusion is ambivalent. On the one hand, I am happy to report such a clear marker of a never-say-die spirit on the part of the writer. On the other hand, I am frustrated at finding one more feature that keeps our purview of his literaturized philosophy and philosophized literature in perpetual suspense, somewhere between the relative pessimism of the central text and the formal openness of the paratexts, though—on balance—this tally exhibits more hope than despair. My belief is that this tilt toward optimism really should surprise no one for, as Tanganelli has pointed out in reference to Unamuno's habitual confrontation of feeling and rationality, "a Unamuno, igual que a tantos otros artistas e intelectuales finiseculares, le interesaba reducir el dominio de lo lógico y abstracto para reivindicar la 'originariedad' de lo patético-concreto" (*Hermenéutica de la crisis* 160). It is a perspective that Unamuno clearly found confirmed in his favorite William James essay, *The Will to Believe*: "Our passional nature not only lawfully may, but must, decide an opinion between propositions, whenever it is a genuine option that cannot by its nature be decided on intellectual grounds" (11).

Those convinced that Unamuno can be rehabilitated only by focusing on his linguistic, narratological, or epistemological innovations at the expense of his commitment to personal survival will, axiomatically, not agree with my bothering to point out the entirety of what I see. In answer to them, I say with Barrett—himself commenting on the tendency to sanitize Unamuno of all existential validity—that to request such an empirical perspective of Unamuno's experience of reality is to cavalierly "step out of that life, to look at it from a distance that would destroy it; to see something he lives as one objective item of fact among others in a class of beliefs" (278). I ask for a minimum of tolerance, for my own stance is more moderate and my conclusions less ontologically definitive for human experience than they might at first seem. What my conclusions ultimately support and restate is Tanganelli's discovery that, in the crises of Unamuno and his Modernist culture, "la teatralidad y la fabulación son calidades inalienables del ser humano" (*Unamuno fin de siglo* 161). My contention is that Unamuno uses the fabulation in his paratexts to put an optimistic or, at very least, an ambiguous and thus a yet undetermined face on what otherwise might be tragic. My unprovable suspicion is that Unamuno justifies this reconfiguration or twisting of his central text according to the same logic with which he repeatedly states (*Vida de Don Quijote y Sancho*) that a work eventually can turn out to be better than the solitary competency of its author. If the interface between the work-in-progress and the imagined reader can produce inexplicable changes or improvements in the work, the interaction of the central text with the author-as-reader can produce second conceptions that might be worthy alternatives or even improvements on the experiences and ideas lending form to the work at earlier stages.

In the examination of Unamuno's fiction carried out in his encyclopedic *Las máscaras de lo trágico: Filosofía y tragedia en Unamuno* (1996), Cerezo, too, uncovers the positive underside of Unamuno's tragic narrative mask. Cerezo finds this optimistic thread even in the central text. Joaquín's envy in *Abel Sánchez* (1917) represents his "herostratic" quest for eternity (614-15). U. Jugo de la Raza's contrary impulses both to continue reading and to cease reading Balzac's deadly novel, when laid next to "Unamuno"'s dual option of immersing himself in history and trying to stand above it—in *Cómo se hace una novela* (1926, 1927)—give narrative testimony to a hedging of bets about survival tactics (674-80). Don Sandalio, the eponymous subject of his own novella (1933), schemes to render "objective" the results of his game of endless configurations (734). Don Emeterio of *Un pobre hombre rico, o el sentimiento cómico de la vida* (1933) sidesteps commitment in order to keep his ontological possibilities open (735-738). In all of these places, Cerezo uncovers the positive dimension of the uncertainty that *Del sentimiento trágico de la vida* hyperbolically (and, in a consummate irony), most hopefully overstates as "trágico," and he does this by focusing on the positive dimension of the deceptively "tragic" central text. Pérez López (63-89) goes beyond this, demonstrating how Unamuno's fictional paradoxes necessarily move in incompatible directions, rational and vital, a situation in which the rational and rectilinear destroys itself in a burst of its own absurdity, leaving a wide field of possibilities connoting a posture of complete relativism. The present study, somewhat differently, fully acknowledges both the positive and the negative sides of the "story"and tries to show how the writer uses the paratext to tip the balance to produce an artificial (in an etymologically pure sense of this word) justification of a primeval, fulfillable will-to-exist-eternally that can, in actuality, never be proved. To coin an analogy, if, as Maíz (*De París a Salamanca*) maintains, during a certain period, Spanish-American intellectuals arrived at an understanding of Parisian culture and their own national realities as these were mediated by Unamuno, the reader of Unamuno's contentious narrative texts comes to interiorize the latter such as they are conditioned by their paratexts.

This "optimistic" mediation—as I have styled it—doubtless can present a vision of Unamuno as an intellectual reactionary afraid or unwilling to entertain a more sobering and perhaps more courageous view of life more in tune with the scientific and philosophical foundations of the contemporary world. Applying what Mermall has said of the more transparent optimism of the essayist Laín Entralgo, we might also say of Unamuno's paratexts that they present an implied "teoriá de la esperanza basada sobre el concepto de la expectativa humana como la estructura ontológica de la existencia" and that, moreover, Unamuno is guilty of failing to give "respuestas con suficiente vigor intelectual a los imperativos culturales de nuestro tiempo," preferring to offer instead an "apología de una concepción [religiosa] del mundo que se derrumbó" (*La retórica* 62). William James himself criticizes thinkers who proceed without caution, who "let belief follow recklessly upon lively conception, especially when the conception has instinctive liking at its back" (x). In the context of Unamunian forms that are novelistic rather than expository, one might well respond to James with Emerson's contention in his essay on "The Over-Soul" that there are inspired moments of art that lift one out of prosaic thinking. "Our faith comes in moments. [...] Yet there is a depth in those moments, which constrains us to ascribe more reality to them than to all other experiences" (Kranzfelder 86). The current volume has no intention of supporting or attacking such suggestions, which many of Unamuno's readers have already advanced and challenged countless times. It is, of course, the ultimate question, the one that really matters, but remains entirely outside the province of a book on narrative paratexts.

Given the prevalent—but false—contention that Unamuno rejected careful structuring and form in favor of complete spontaneity, total irony, parody, and an unbegrudging openendedness, even when dealing novelistically with matters of human mortality, I feel compelled to provide a theoretical framework that may serve to bridge the gap between this study's formalist—therefore, structurally enclosed—convictions and the organicism and concomitant polyvalency justifiably highlighted by others such as La Rubia Prado (29-63) and Vauthier ("Introduction" 13-129). I borrow my framework in part from John Dewey, the American pragmatist philosopher, a thinker Unamuno knew well enough to justify the perception of many parallels between his own ontology and that of his contemporary.

In *Art as Experience* (1934), an application to art of the principles in his better-known earlier work, Dewey stresses the need to apprehend visual art, music, and literature, not primarily as the product of an isolating interpretive tradition, as Fish (*Is There a Text in this Class?*) would have it, but as the creation of an intense, highly interactive experience shared by artist (writer) and perceiver (reader). The perceiver and artist, in turn, are the locus of a unique psyche and a specific moment in the development of society. Works of art and literature are not artifacts to be preserved in some museum but spiritualizing and intellectualizing reflections on everyday lives. Art crystalizes the most important combinations of emotions and ideas that human beings associate with the social commerce of their living. Anyone who has read the artistic pronouncements of the philosopher Entrambosmares in Unamuno's *Amor y pegagogía* (1902) or chapter 7 of *Del sentimiento trágico de la vida* (1912)—and the relevant sections from the *Tratado del amor de Dios* (1906-1908) that have been reworked to form it—will recognize that Unamuno shared this belief in an individual/societal locus for art. Throughout his entire life, Unamuno, like Dewey, William James, and other pragmatists, rejected any notion of "art for art's sake." His early and never-completely-forgotten Marxism made him lament the progressive reduction of art—whose origins he perceived as demotic—to mechanically-reproduced artifices that glorified *in aeternum* the tenets of a particular economic system. He thus stands as a critical precursor, albeit a distant one, of Foucault's conviction (*The Order of Things*) that modern writing callously abandoned its reflection of natural signs for the arbitrary creation of signs of its own as well as of Jameson's demonstrations (*Postmodernism*) that the arts have become a semiological means to glorify international capitalism. Dewey (9-10) maintains that the progressive formalism and eccentricity of modern art is the natural response of the artist to his or her gradual marginalization from a position of influence in everyday society and isolation from the true, life-giving origins of art. We might include the esoteric nature of some of

Unamuno's own writing—the outlandish claims to "viviparous" composition, the *nivola*, the reduction of narrative to allegory, the almost suffocating—at times—reliance on paradox and chiasmus—in this indictment of attention-getting strategies in an age when humanism is no longer king. Certainly Unamuno's work does have this aspect, but it is, in the final result, I think, absolved from the thrust of these criticisms by the serious purpose that the present study induces from a study of his narrative paratexts: the formal creation of an ontological edifice that reserves some hope for life beyond death.

Dewey maintained that, in art, "Form is arrived at whenever a stable, even though moving, equilibrium is reached." He goes on to state: "Wherever there is this coherence, there is endurance. Order is not imposed from without but is made out of the relations of harmonious interactions that energies bear to one another" (14). Furthermore, "[O]nly when an organism shares in the ordered relations of its environment does it secure the stability essential to living. And when the participation comes after a phase of disruption and conflict, it bears within itself the germs of a consummation akin to the esthetic" (15). Art consists of the "rhythm of loss of integration and recovery of union." "Emotion is the conscious sign of a break, actual or impending. The discord is the occasion that induces reflection. Desire for restoration of the union converts mere emotion into interest in objects as conditions of realization of harmony."

In the recent past, the vogue of chaos theory popularized the dichotomy between the simultaneous chaos and order of the universe. At the same time, the rise of Bakhtinian formalism introduced terms like "dialogy" and "dialogical" in reference to discursive streams that were initially at loggerheads but ultimately—through a regularization and interpenetration of their patterns—came to produce a dialogue from which the reader might extract one or more synthetic equations. In both cases an initial disorder was rendered more ordered through the human ability—or, as Unamuno might say, predisposition—to perceive an overreaching pattern or process of unity. Nowhere does Don Miguel state this position better than in poem 63 of his *Cancionero* (composed 1928-1936):

> No te devanes los sesos
> buscando al mundo razón;
> es un devaneo vano;
> devánate el corazón.
>
> El corazón es ovillo
> que nos regaló el Amor;
> las raíces de la vida
> le abrazan en derredor.
> (5: 114)

This is essentially what happens in Unamuno's fiction. His narratives, which, as Marías states (50-54), primarily deal with a single obsessive question—the fate of human personality after death—dramatize multiple, violently contradictory means of dealing with this problem. Eventually, these contradictory but endlessly reiterated strands produce a ceaseless dialogue that leaves the reader without closure. This lack of closure creates a space for hope. Maybe some human being will, through further play like that of Unamuno's principal characters, hit upon a new ontological scheme that confirms the hopes of characters and reader alike. At the same time, both characters and reader are highly cognizant that they, like the often-present "Unamuno," are only playing games, punning, willfully ignoring absurd flaws in their plan. This inextinguishable knowledge of a badly camouflaged assent to equivocation leads ultimately to a concomitant, perhaps overriding pessimism. At the very least, it leads back to skepticism. The perspective put forward in the present study is that it is by means of his paratexts that Unamuno tips the balance in favor of continued hope but that this weighting of the scale is not a dishonest imposition of the author's slight of hand but the logical effect upon the narrative of the longings and silent, metaphysical underpinnings ("Since you seek me, you have already found me") of characters and reader, ensconced as they are in the skeptical but still Judeo-Christian society in which Unamuno lived and in which he immerses them. This is the *episteme* with which Unamuno always works, but it is clearly also a gestalt rife with discontinuities and ruptures that are always inherent in it. (The language is borrowed from Foucault, but Unamuno's antecedence, reflecting perhaps Darwinian and Schopenhauerian notions of discontinuous evolution, is present in all of his major essays.) Human search for an apologetics of perpetuity leads to skepticism and even despair, but despair launches a worldview of absurdity, and the latter rather startlingly breeds hope. It is through this rhythmic, regularizing frustration and re-enabling of the quest for a substantiation of perpetual continuity of the personality that Unamuno's fiction creates the illusion of organic stability that serves to undergird the seemingly quaint Pascalian "logic" suggesting that human longings and societal commonplaces are reasonable harbingers of truth. Dewey—certainly no apologist for God—arrives at a similar, existential/Platonic sense of human permanence: "through the phases of perturbation and conflict, there abides the deep-seated memory of an underlying harmony, the sense of which haunts life like the sense of being founded on a rock" (17). It is art that enables one to move from this intuition to its veritable substantiation in one's own intimate experience: "The existence of art […] is proof that man uses the materials and energies of nature *with intent* to expand his own life" (25; emphasis mine). Once expanded, even eternalized through art, the thus created artifice of life not only is grasped as authentic but interacts with the rest of the environment so as to fundamentally re-create the individual or society that, in interaction with the surroundings, had in fact created it (59-67). From this it will be appreciated that for Dewey and Unamuno, as for Zubiri, reality is an oscillating structure whose independent parts are independently predisposed to an interactive affinity (*Estructura dinámica de la realidad*, chs. 3-5) that authorizes the extrapolation of dynamic laws or—in prose fiction—evolving paratextual parameters.

I have chosen to discuss Unamuno's use of paratexts in the same order that Genette lists and theorizes about their uses. That is, I have not created individual chapters to label and analyze the importance of paratextual material in each of Unamuno's novels and novellas. I have preferred instead to discuss in separate units all of Unamuno's uses of prologues, of epilogues, of notes, and of other paratextual elements. I have done this so that the reader might gain a meaningful grasp of the extremely wide-ranging use of each paratextual type in Unamuno's fiction. It is only by exploring such units independently that one learns which paratexts best accommodate themselves to Unamuno's technique. It is also through this type of segregation that the reader best prepares to apply my limited perceptions to paratexts I may have missed; paratexts that I (either wisely or foolishly) left out, judging them largely irrelevant; paratexts in other Unamunian genres; and differing interpretations of the central text. From this it becomes clear that I view the present contribution more as a useful handbook or introduction than as any final word. I also want to make clear my conviction that Unamuno's fiction cannot be limited to its paratexts, much less to any theory about how the paratexts work. A narrative is many things, and its paratexts are only one of them , though—in the case of Unamuno's major narratives—the paratextual dimension is clearly more important than it is in the fiction of most other writers. Even then, to *completely* explore the functioning of the paratextual features in any given Unamuno narrative it would be necessary to point out every instance in which the central text (in its final attachment to the paratexts) alludes—in either ambiguously supportive or ambiguously contradictory ways—to the paratextual features in even their more superficial ontological implications. This would involve us in a maze of associations that are best left to the resolution of the individual reader, that is, to the resolution of the prodded but not unduly regimented co-creator that both text and paratext suppose. This volume can only serve as a guide—one informed person's guide—to that end.

Principal Paratexts of Unamuno's Narratives

(Dates, with the exception of *Nuevo mundo*, refer to first publication. Unamuno readily admits that many of the prologues listed here are—in date of composition—actually postlogues. This study considers both position in the text and moment of composition.)

Nuevo mundo (1896)

Potential place of publication
Potential date of publication
Transcriber's prologue
Essay that Eugenio Rodero left among his papers
Notes and memoirs that Rodero bequeathed to the transcriber
More notes
"Gabriel" (narrative insertion in which Rodero appears under different name)
"Eugenio" (narrative insertion)
Diario íntimo
Cómo se hace una novela
Correspondence

Paz en la guerra (1897)

Date of publication
Place of publication
Notice of printing errors (removed from many later editions)

Prologue to second edition
Paratexts to other narratives
Diario íntimo

Amor y pedagogía (1902)

Niebla

Dedication
Publisher
Place of Publication
Prologue to first edition
Prologue-epilogue to second edition
Epilogue
Notes on the art of paper bird-making
Transcriber's note on essay on the art of paper bird-making
Index (appears only in first edition)
Appendix
Transcriber's note on appendix
Diario íntimo
Correspondence
Paratexts to other narratives

Niebla (1914)

Amor y pedagogía

Publication date
Publisher
Prologue
Post-prologue
Prologue to third edition ("Historia de *Niebla*")
Footnote in chapter 13
Internal note in chapter 25
Epilogue ("Oración fúnebre")

Fictional reprises of Augusto and "Unamuno"
Paratexts to other narratives
Diario íntimo
Cómo se hace una novela

Abel Sánchez (1917)

Publisher
Transcriber's note
Final exclamation
Paratexts to other narratives
Correspondence

La tía Tula (1920)

Publisher
Prologue
Paratexts to other prologues
Correspondence

Tres novelas ejemplares y un prólogo (1921). Includes *Dos madres, El marqués de Lumbría, Nada menos que todo un hombre* (1916)

Publisher
Publication dates of individual works
Prologue
Paratexts to other narratives
Correspondence

Cómo se hace una novela (1926, 1927)

Places of publication
Dates of publication
Epigraph to prologue
Prologue
Portrait of Unamuno

Commentary
Bracketed comments/extensions (1927 edition)
Continuation (1927 edition)
Continuation of Continuation (1927 edition)
Paratexts to other narratives

San Manuel Bueno, mártir y tres historias más (1933). Includes *San Manuel Bueno, mártir* (1931), *La novela de Don Sandalio, jugador de ajedrez, Un pobre hombre rico, o el sentimiento cómico de la vida, Una historia de amor* (1911)

Publisher
Publication dates
Prologue
Appendix to prologue
Epigraph to *San Manuel Bueno, mártir*
Prologue-like paragraph to *San Manuel Bueno, mártir*
Epilogue to *San Manuel Bueno, mártir*
Epigraph to *La novela de Don Sandalio*
Prologue to *La novela de Don Sandalio*
Internal note to chapter 15 of *La novela de Don Sandalio*
Epilogue to *La novela de Don Sandalio*
Epigraph to *Un pobre hombre rico*
Epilogue or postlogue to *Un pobre hombre rico*
Paratexts to other narratives
Correspondence

OTHER PARATEXTS DISCUSSED

Teresa (1924)

Preface
Prologue
Notes
Postlogue

De Fuerteventura a París (1925)
Prologue
Explanatory notes

NOTE: With the exception of the paratexts to *Nuevo mundo* and *Cómo se hace una novela*, the second edition prologue to *Abel Sánchez*, and the many discussions of the printing peculiarities found in the first editions, all page references to Unamuno's narrative are from *Obras Completas*, ed. Ricardo Senabre, 5 vols. (Madrid: Turner, 1995-2003). For *Teresa* and *De Fuerteventura a París* I have used *Poesía Completa*, ed. Ana Suárez de Miramón, 4 vols. (Madrid: Alianza, 1987-1989) because it includes paratexts left out of both the Senabre and the García Blanco *Obras Completas*.

1
Texts and Paratexts in the Unamunian Style

IN A STATEMENT THAT is by now famous, Genette defines paratexts as the "liminal devices [...] that mediate the relations between text and reader" (xi). When Genette speaks of the text, he refers to the central body of the text—the text minus its preceding and succeding additions. These additions or paratextual devices include titles, signs of authorship, dedications, epigraphs, prefaces, prologues, notes and all the "literary and printerly conventions that mediate between the world of publishing and the world of the text" (xvii). Paratexts, according to Genette, "surround" and "extend" a text, "precisely in order to *present* it [...] to insure the text's presence in the world, its 'reception' and consumption in the form [...] of a book" (1). They represent an "'undefined zone' between the "inside and the outside" of a book, a vehicle for deciding whether to enter or to turn back (2). Not all paratexts are of the same order. Some (prospectuses, prepublication announcements) were created prior to the completion of the book, while others were written after the book was finished (these are the vast majority) or even after it was published (introductions to subsequent editions). Paratexts are sometimes metatextual and hypertextual, meaning that they both establish links between themselves and the text to which they are appended and that they change the complexion of the central text by imitating, parodying, or creating a pastiche of it (xix).

All of Unamuno's novelistic hypertexts are linked to their

narratives, though some—the introductions to *Tres novelas ejemplares* and *San Manuel Bueno, mártir y tres historias más*—establish very weak relationships, occasioned by the the commercial need to provide an umbrella for what are largely independent works. The author may, indeed, try to devise some sort of justification for publishing the works together—for example, "el pavoroso problema de la personalidad" (*OC* 2: 307) in *San Manuel Bueno, mártir y tres historias más*—, and some critics might agree (Olson, *The Great Chiasmus* 175), but such justifications in and of themselves seem largely "traídas de los pelos." Some of this awkwardness in *San Manuel Bueno, mártir y tres historias más* may be deliberate, as illustrated by the large spaces that in the first edition separate the original prologue dated 1932; its supplementary discussion of *Una historia de amor*, included in the collection at the very last moment; the commentary on the character Liduvina in this work, a commentary dated 1933; the epigraph to *San Manuel Bueno, mártir*; the form of the latter work, headed by its epigraph and followed by its epilogue; *Un pobre hombre rico o El sentimiento cómico de la vida* (the definite article capitalized to create a contrast with Unamuno's famous philosophical essay having a similar title), headed by its epigraph from the Song of Songs and followed by its postlogue, dated 1930; and *Una historia de amor*, sans its inconvenient 1911 date. All of this confused dating, agglomerizing, and deliberate spacing of the parts cleverly and self-consciously suggests a vitality and a creativity out of control.

The author of a paratext may be the actual author, a fictionalized "author," another character invented by the author, or a third party. For Criado Miguel (81, 94-95), the authors of Unamuno's paratexts and his narrators are thinly disguised mouthpieces for the actual author who wishes to find a literarily acceptable manner to participate discursively on the diegetic level of his fiction. This, as I will show, is often true when one focuses on the philosophical dimension of Unamuno's narratives, but it seems to me that the detection of such an interior implicit author destroys much of the play—and the philosophy—that abounds in the narratives if one additionally accepts the paratextual writers as—with a few complex exceptions—largely autonomous entities.

The second prologuist to *Cómo se hace una novela*, Jean Cassou, is the only representative of the third-party, historical paratextualist to be found in Unamuno's narratives, though our perception of him is shaped largely by a following commentary inserted in the name of the author. The prologue to *Niebla*, on the other hand, is offered as the work of one of the novel's characters, while the post-prologue is the creation of a fictionalized "Unamuno" also appearing within the text. The essay on the art of paper bird-making appended to *Amor y pedagogía* is the work of one of the novel's characters, the philosopher Entrambosmares. The prologues to *Nuevo mundo* and *Abel Sánchez* are attributed to transcribers of the multiple strands of text that they have inherited from various oral and written sources. The epilogue to *Niebla* is attributed to the protagonist's dog, introduced by a narrative voice attributable to either Víctor or "Unamuno." Unamuno uses no pseudonymous authors under the titles of his novels, but he can be said to use pseudonymous prologuists and epiloguists. This is because, beneath the prologues attributed to such paratextualists as Fulgencio Entrambosmares (*Amor y pedagogía*), Víctor Goti (*Niebla*), and the transcribers of *Nuevo mundo* and *Abel Sánchez*, one easily detects a hyperbolic, almost parodic foregrounding of the ideas and expository voicing of Miguel de Unamuno. In these cases, I think that the Unamuno = paratextualist equation established by Criado proves partially correct. The hyberbolic-parodic nature of the paratexts creates an intermediate zone in which they are neither slavish mouthpieces for the author's own ideas nor an entity totally separate from them. Unamuno, therefore, does not sheepishly use his paratexts to disassociate himself from the controversial content of his central texts, a fact clearly discernible in the discussions of pornography in the prologues to *Niebla* and *San Manuel Bueno, mártir y tres historias más*. This practice runs parallel to the onymity or "author"-alluding nature (Genette 39-41) of his protagonists. U. Jugo de la Raza, as the etymologizing narrator of *Cómo se hace una novela* makes clear, is really a partial double of the narrative's true protagonist, the fictional "Miguel de Unamuno." The seemingly anonymous protagonist-letter writer of *La novela de Don Sandalio*, is, as "Unamuno" the epiloguist avers, a creation of his own pen. This transparency is, as the Balzac whose *Colonel Chabert* (Franz, "*Abel Sánchez y Le Colonel Chabert*" 408-13) and *La peau de chagrin* (Olson, *The Great Chiasmus* 158) are intertextual with *Abel Sánchez* and *Cómo se hace una novela*, makes clear, a sign of the modesty of one who would demystify his own creative powers (Genette 44). This is particularly true when the psuedonymous paratextualist supplies a rich assortment of his author-specific concrete attributes (47). If *Niebla*'s Augusto Pérez and Eugenia Domingo del Arco can reflect the casino habitués and the symbolic importance of the piano in turn-of-the-century Salamanca society (Kent 25, 27, 99), the paratextualists and protagonists can also mime—but not duplicate with reliable exactitude—the ideas and developmental stages of the historical Unamuno.

In view of Genette's indication that such author-specific details are invariably signs of weakly "disguised autobiographies" (41), we should not shy away, as we have over the past thirty years, from identifying Unamuno's novels with a certain hyperbolic treatment of parts of his own personal evolution. Psycho-biographical interpreters such as Abellán, Feal, Jurkevich, López-Marrón, Fox, and Sinclair have merely foregrounded a focus that Unamuno himself had privileged. The question is whether the application of a Freudian, Jungian, or Lacanian lens has the necessary flexibility to see around the degree of parodic distortion that Unamuno has inserted in order to allay his own anxieties about the reader's detection of autobiographical perceptions. It seems to me that Jung's focus on developmental processes, Freud's mechanisms for seeing behind conscious manipulation, and Lacan's insights into self-projections in the process of personal definition give the critic a means of getting beyond Unamuno's many masks and distortions. However, to move beyond them without an even more deliberate consideration of the mechanisms and semiotics of the distortions themselves is to wipe out a great deal of Unamuno's narratives as art. The form and discourse of the story itself is just as important as its psychic or allegorical dimensions, and we await a study that shows how Unamuno's particular language is a key to unlocking the underlying psychological processes of his fiction. De Kock's (*Introducción* 123-32), Mermall's ("The Chiasmus" passim) and Olson's ("Sobre las estructuras," *The Great Chiasmus*, both passim) studies of chiasmus are important steps in this direction, and doubtless there are many insights to be gained from further work with Lacan.

Genette (24-26) speaks of a publisher's peritext, paratextual items that are historically the province of the publisher rather than of the author, among which we find the genre indicator and the cover illustration. The unfortunate illustrations by Penagos included in the original 1931 edition of *San Manuel Bueno, mártir* (Unamuno had rejected the editor Valentí Camp's suggestion that one Álvarez Dumont, a serious rather than a comic artist, be permitted to illustrate the tragicomic *Amor y pedagogía* [Vauthier, *Arte de escribir* 339-40]) were certainly not instigated by Unamuno but by *La Novela de Hoy*'s director, Pedro Sáinz Rodríguez, who clearly wanted to highlight key moments in the passage of narrative time. The narrative, however, undercuts such a notion of time, as the diegetic "Unamuno" makes clear in the final section:

> Bien sé que en lo que se cuenta en este relato no pasa nada; mas espero que sea porque en ello todo se queda, como se quedan los lagos y las montañas y las santas almas sencillas asentadas más allá de la fe y de la desesperación, que en ellos, en los lagos y las montañas, fuera de la historia, en la divina novela, se cobijan. (2: 346)

Except for its allusions to Kierkegaard and Marx and the attempt to unionize agricultural labor in Spain, the narrative is practically timeless. Nevertheless, the illustrator depicts the adult Ángela as a sophisticated woman in a 1930s' suit. As an adolescent she is represented in a habit, as if she were a postulant. The text, on the other hand, states only that wshe was a residential student at a convent school. In his sketch, Blasillo, the holy fool, bears all the grotesque marks of a Quasimodo or a Rigoletto. The young Don Manuel sports the grotesque hat of a citified cowboy. The sixth illustration presents Don Manuel at about forty years of age. In the next drawing he has some very visible gray hair. The following one shows him as a worn-out old man with a snowy crown. Yet this diachronicity is very secondary in the narrative, which is as much an intrahistoric prose poem as a story. No wonder Unamuno decided to republish the narrative only two years later as the title piece in *San Manuel Bueno, mártir y tres historias más*: he had to wrest control of his text from illustrator who had handed it to the reader in a very different form. One should never discount the influence of the illustrator on the reader's multilayerd appropriation of an illustrated work (Miller 101-07). Despite the incongruency of Unamuno's text and the publisher's peritext in the original edition of *San Manuel*, elsewhere in Unamuno's narratives we encounter a marked divergence from the traditional separation of the textual and visual responsibilities or of the text and the arrangement of the title page. The cover illustrator for one of the latter's most famous narratives, *Abel Sánchez*, was Unamuno himself, and in the prologue to the second edition to the novel he states that the gloomy cover he prepared (reproduced on p. 179 of *El tiempo de Miguel de Unamuno y Salamanca*) was responsible for the dismal sales of the first edition. While it is true that the publisher of *Paz en la guerra* placed the word "novela" beneath the title in editions after the first, it was Unamuno who included the designation "(Nivola)" under the title *Niebla*, added the almost naturalistic subtitle "Una historia de pasión" to *Abel Sánchez*, and inserted the Cervantine designator "novelas" in *Tres novelas ejemplares*. Even at the beginning of Unamuno's narrative career we find this sort of thing. What today's scholars usually refer to as *Paz en la guerra* was originally *Paz en la Guerra*, the capital letter distinctly suggesting Tolstoy's conceptual balance in *War and Peace*. It appears that with Unamuno these narrative indicators are in every way hints of the type of narrative that follows. Words like "nivola" or an absence of indicator cue the reader to expect the unexpected, whereas words like "novela" (*Paz en la guerra* and *La tía Tula* in their original editions or *La novela de Don Sandalio*) and "historia," (*Abel Sánchez, Una historia de amor*) a capital letter (*Paz en la Guerra* and *San Manuel Bueno, Mártir* in their first editions), or a title based on a protagonist's name (*Abel Sánchez, La tía Tula, San Manuel Bueno, mártir, La novela de Don Sandalio*) point one back to the neater focuses and formalistic structure of nineteenth-century narrative. It is significant that the title *Cómo se hace una novela* points in both directions, the word "novela" (as opposed to "nivola") pointing to the past, while the reflexive "se hace" negates that past and suggests the vitalism of Ortega and the literary vanguard of the moment.

Genette asks the important question as to "whom" these so-called publisher's peritexts and other types of paratexts really address. It is usually assumed that they address readers who have bought and read (or are about to read) the book (75). But this is not necessarily the case, for many people buy books that they do not read, or that they read poorly or only partially. Unamuno's paratexts are clearly antithetical to these latter types of reader, since they talk against them. The prologue and epilogue to *Amor y pedagogía*, when taken together, tell two stories—one of an apocryphal customer and the writer "Unamuno," the other of an "editor" (simulacrum of Santiago Valentí Camp, the representative of the Barcelona publisher Henrich, who brought out the first edition of Unamuno's novel) who demanded that books in a series be all of equal size, so that the non-reading "reader," who only bought the books to display them, would have his home-decorating fantasies realized (*OC* 1: 311-12; Vauthier, "Epistolario" 458-65). Víctor Goti's prologue to *Niebla* approvingly quotes "Unamuno"'s attacks against readers who want to laugh at a novel in order to better digest their food (1: 473), while the prologue to *La tía Tula* carries the ironic concession "(Que puede saltar el lector de novelas)" (1: 797), which of course is not true, given its only *seemingly* tongue-in-cheek directions for a feminist reading of the work.

There can be a wide discrepancy between the reader addressed in the title and the reader inferred from the work (Genette 75). That is, the title may make the work sound either more or less intellectual, complex, or poetic than the work actually is. Some Unamuno titles deliver what they they promise (Genette would call these formal titles), but some clearly do not (Genette styles these thematic titles). *Paz en la guerra* sounds Tolstoyan, and much of it is. *Amor y pedagogía* establishes an incongruous juxtaposition that will be jarringly fulfilled by its text. *Una historia de amor* is about love, though its erotic element is soon sublimated into a love of God. *Niebla* suggests that it is avant-garde, and it does not deceive. *Dos Madres* is true to its form, though one of the "mothers" is anything but motherly. *La tía Tula* suggests a character study, though a somewhat more complex and ruthless one than its folksy title might suggest. However, *Nuevo mundo* sounds like geographical exploration or a rendering of contemporary society, but it is neither, but rather the entering of its protagonist Eugenio Rodero into the realm of a structureless, post-theological metaphysics: "Salió del templo respirando nuevas auras y creó entrar en un nuevo mundo" (57). *Nada menos que todo un hombre* surprisingly is not about masculine strength but weakness. *Abel Sánchez* is not about a real man but about the envious fantasy with which Joaquín Monegro obscures him. *El marqués de Lumbría* is not about a man but the will of a woman. *Cómo se hace una novela* seems to be a treatise on writing effective novels and it is in part, but more than this it is a novel about how Unamuno turned his exile into a living legend. *San Manuel Bueno, mártir* gives the appearance that it is the biography of a saint, but it is in reality a piece of fiction about how Manuel Bueno (and doubtless Unamuno himself) courageously (or perhaps hypocritically) projected a degree of religious faith that most people would say that they did not actually have. *La novela de Don Sandalio, jugador de ajedrez* is not about a real-life chess player but about the urge to invent him out of one's own metaphysical and existential needs. It goes without saying that none of these novelistic titles is as monovalent as those of the author's memoirs or essays: *En torno al casticismo, Vida de Don Quijote y Sancho, Recuerdos de niñez y mocedad, Del sentimiento trágico de la vida, La agonía del cristianismo.* Despite Unamuno's frequent equation of biography and philosophy with the writing of fiction and poetry, in his essays—even the most intuitional and freely formed ones—the thematic expectations planted in the title hold sway. The frequent defrauding of these expectations in the course of his narration is a suggestion of the paradoxical effects to which his paratexts are most often calculated to contribute.

2
Dedications and Epigraphs

THE ONLY UNAMUNO NOVEL that has a dedication is *Amor y pedagogía*: "Al lector dedica esta obra El autor" (1: 297), which in the original and most subsequent editions is carefully printed to suggest Unamuno's own handwriting, a manufactured "personal" touch that the author reproduces in the signature "Miguel de Unamuno" that concludes the first edition (1920) of *Tulio Montalbán y Julio Macedo*. Spires (26-35) has underlined the importance of the words of *Amor y pedagogía*'s dedication, for they show the degree to which Unamuno is relying on the reader to pull together this multifaceted novel with its many paratexts. As Spires points out, *Amor y pedagogía* is prelude to the preeminent cocreative role the reader will enjoy in Unamuno's next novel, *Niebla*. Unfortunately, it is not quite clear whether this dedication, which we record immediately below as given in the first edition, is in conformity to Unamuno's ultimate intentions or the true sense of the work. Many editions of the novel reverse subject and object, giving "El autor dedica esta obra al lector." Vauthier's 2002 edition is almost faithful to the 1902 edition, giving "Al Lector, dedica esta obra El Autor" for the original "Al Lector, dedica esta obra, El Autor," but in her book on Unamuno's novelistic irony she adds italics to the words "El Autor" (*Arte de escribir* 334), pointing out that in the 1934 second prologue Unamuno himself chooses to emphasize his own controlling power. (The original title page of *Niebla* lists both Unamuno's [or "Unamuno"'s] name and the title in boldface but relegates the fictional prologuist and implied author, Víctor

Goti, and, by extension, the implied reader for whom he creates, to Roman type). Some editions of *Amor y pedagogía*, following the first edition, capitalize both of these nouns; some do not. If both nouns are capitalized, we have a dedicatory intertext with the Germanic conventions of Thomas Carlyle, upon whose novel *Sartor Resartus* (1833-1834) much of Unamuno's metaliterary concept and characterizations in the 1902 novel are based (Clavería 7-62). This intertwining of the two texts would serve only to reinforce the need to see the novel as part of the anti-abuse-of-education, anti-pedanticsm paradigm formed by Carlyle's novel, Dickens's *Hard Times* (1845), and Galdós's *Torquemada en la hoguera* (1889). If "autor" is to receive the stress, the tragic stories of Avito and Apolodoro Carrascal must be seen against the determinism of an implied author (a symbolic God) who sadistically denies his characters fulfillment of their longing for self-determination (and eternal life). If, on the contrary, "lector" receives the emphasis, the onus for making sense (or eternity) out life falls squarely to the God-like creativity of the reader. Whatever the case, Genette would classify Unamuno's dedication as "factual" rather than "textual" (118) because the dedicatee (the reader) is never mentioned in the novel's text despite Entrambosmares's vision of Aplodoro as a potential corrector of his own plot in chapters 4 and 12. It is only in *Niebla* that the reader is called upon by name — in chapters 31-33 and in the prologue and post-prologue, and, by inference, in the dog's epilogue — to decide whether Augusto's life depends on the whims of "Unamuno" or whether "Unamuno" depends on the reader's internalization of the suffering of "Unamuno"'s character. The reader is thus cast into a receptive stance (as participant) to incline toward the view of his own vital importance in the work.

Genette caustically remarks that "One may [...] simply (too simply, perhaps) dedicate to the reader" (133), a criticism that has a certain validity with *Amor y pedagogía*, unless one understands Unamuno's "reader" as being, at some point or other, Unamuno himself, in perpetual dialogue with his own text. Unamuno may thus decide to endlessly alter his provisional current "reading" of his in-progress novel by appending further paratexts. This is what he will eventually do with the many paratextual additions to *Niebla* and to *Cómo se hace una novela*. As Robles has shown (37-39), this is also what Unamuno apparently was on the way to doing with his abandoned and only recently published *Nuevo mundo*, which doubtless served as his laboratory for the idea. Genette points out (142) that in rare instances an author will mistakenly dedicate a work to a second party after initially dedicating it to someone else (as when a novel or poem receives a dedication in a periodical and mistakenly receives another when the work is published in a collection, or when the author authorizes a formal, printed dedication but afterword pens in a spontaneous one [Genette terms this an inscription] to a friend more immediately on the author's mind). The evolution of the identity of the reader between *Amor y pedagogía* and *Niebla* may perhaps be seen in this light. At first the reader is anyone who will or could be imagined to look at the text, perhaps not even a concrete or performative reader. Then Unamuno sees how a reader (perhaps himself) can engage with the otherness of his creation and nuzzle it onward to a progressively more auspicious metaphysical resolution. Finally, he imagines a reader like *Niebla*'s upon whom he bestows the privilege of standing in for himself in the God-like role of one who may fiddle with the text in ways that would violate the author's own commitments to diegetical and philosophical consistency. Genette theorizes that ownership of the penned-in inscription (Unamuno's empowering of himself in the role of reader) may give the text unique powers to influence the possessing subject, but it also devalues the printed text itself by implying that its paramount value lies not in its universal readability but in its possession (142-43). This reasoning suggests that what Unamuno achieves by literary slight of hand may devalue consideration of his literature as "mere" literaturized philosophy.

Genette speculates that today's prose narratives inherited their epigraphs from the gothic novel (146). If that is the case, it is strange that the one Unamuno narrative having many gothic characteristics—*Abel*

Sánchez (Franz, "*Abel Sánchez* and Wilde's")—comes without an epigraph. Indeed, no Unamuno novel carries an epigraph until the 1926 initial (and much shorter) French version—*Comment on fait un roman*—of *Cómo se hace una novela*. Thereafter, *San Manuel Bueno, mártir, Un pobre hombre rico o el sentimiento cómico de la vida* (Unamuno is notoriously inconsistent about capitalizing the *e* in the *El* of the title), and *La novela de Don Sandalio* have epigraphs. One might conjecture that the appearance of epigraphs at this time is tied to Unamuno's 1924-1930 French exile and his extensive reading of French works. Ouimette has done us a favor by detailing the degree to which the most famous of Unamuno's works of exile, the philosophical essay *La agonía del cristianismo*—also appearing first in French translation (*L'Agonie du christianisme*) before the appearance of the original Spanish version—is constructed with building blocks salvaged from French literature, philosophy, and the reporting of political events in the French press (Ouimette 9-62). *Cómo se hace una novela* speaks a great deal about both Paris and the Basque area of France, for it is in these places that the novel's protagonist, "Unamuno" and his double, U. Jugo de la Raza, contemplate the meaning of their highly literary lives against the equally literary backdrop of history.

In the novel, U. Jugo de La Raza buys a copy of Balzac's *La peau de chagrin* (1831), begins to identify intensely with its character, and comes to a page where the narrator informs the character that the shagreen skin he has found will shrink every time he relies on its magic text to enhance or prolong his own life. Because the character's life is tied to the content of the shrinking text, Jugo de la Raza intuits that he too will die if he continues to read the enthralling volume to the end. La Raza continues reading, because, through the very reading process, he has become one with the protagonist of the novel and, therefore, feels propelled by the thrust of the former's experience. Just as the Balzacian character will, in effect die, when he finishes off the text on the *peau de chagrin*, La Raza will die at the end of the Balzac novel. To save his life, La Raza burns Balzac's book, but shortly afterward feels compelled through an irresistible identification with Balzac's parallel character to buy another copy. In addition to this drawn-out intertext with Balzac, there are many references to Mirabeau, Victor Hugo, Proust, Gide, and Flaubert, making the literary atmosphere quite French. It is a literary atmosphere that is, to be precise, quite philosophical, though far less so than that of *La agonía del cristianismo*.

Unamuno never shied away from epigraphs with his philosophical writings nor with his more philosophical poems, and we might assume that the French setting of *Cómo se hace una novela* automatically put Unamuno in a philosophical frame of mind. (We need to remember that *Cómo se hace una novela* takes up the same issue—whether it is possible to escape the certainty of mortality through a fictional game of diegetic planes—that is the crux of the author's most clearly philosophical narratives, *Amor y pedagogía* and *Niebla*.) Someone will inevitably object that these two earlier novels have no epigraph, which is true, but they have something similar that falls outside the field of the paratext. They have extensive philosophical intertexts with works of Descartes, Kant, Hegel, Kierkegaard, Schopenhauer, Nietzsche, and many other important thinkers. An epigraph above all is an intertext. It sets up the broader context in which the work is intended to be read. It appears that the epigraph to *Cómo se hace una novela*—the sketchiest, most formalistic, and conceptual of Unamuno's narratives—signals that the work is to be read, not as a story, nor as a an exemplum of novel writing (an "exemplary novel," as Unamuno would term such fiction in the prologue to his *Tres novelas ejemplares*) but as an exercise in philosophy. Indeed, Olson's diagnosis of a deliberate contradiction between the "closed" ending of the 1926 version, and the decidedly "open" version of the progressive set of 1927 "endings" (*The Great Chiasmus* 159-60) points toward a dialectic in which the reader is left hanging to make weighty epistemological and ontological decisions. Such a need to make decisions is but the natural outcome of a dynamic, autobiographically-charged self-questioning text that recent critics have successfully related to the non-Spanish tradition of the literary confession and the diary

(Marichal, "La originalidad" 49-78; Vauthier, "El *Manual de quijotismo*" 27-45).

The epigraph to *Cómo se hace una novela* to which much of the foregoing has been directed is "Mihi quaestio factus sum," a quote from the *Confessions* (bk X, ch. 33, 50) of Saint Augustine which suggests that the self inevitably becomes the starting point for all human inquiry. This philosophical-theological note is continued in the epigraph to *San Manuel Bueno, mártir*: "Si sólo en esta vida esperamos en Cristo, somos los más miserables de los hombres todos" (2: 313) which originates in Saint Paul (1 Cor. 15:19). (For Unamuno, "quien dice [producción] novelesca [...] dice filosófica y teológica" [prologue to the 1933 four-novella compendium].) The quote not only leads one to suspect that the novel's protagonist, the priest Manuel Bueno, will eventually reveal a disbelief in the eternal life but to conjecture that the novel surreptitiously deals with both the Kantian conflict of the phenomenon and the noumenon and the Pascalian dichotomy of the mind and the heart. The epigraph suggests that the Christ-figure protagonist re-enacts a philosophical problem present in the mind of Jesus himself and, to Unamuno's authorial mind, intuited by Saint Paul. Sánchez Barbudo has theorized that the *histoire* for Unamuno's treatment of a doubting priest also comes from a French source: the "Profession de foi du vicaire savoyard" section of Rousseau's philosophical-pedagogical novel *Émile* (M.C. de Unamuno 194-95).

The third Unamuno novel with an epigraph is *La novela de Don Sandalio, jugador de ajedrez*, whose epigraph comes from Flaubert's *Bouvard et Pécuchet*. It reads: "Alors, une faculté pitoyable se développa dans leur esprit, celle de voir la bêtise et de ne plus la tolérer"(2: 349). It is a motif that the work will echo repeatedly, as the unnamed letter writer informs his friend Felipe about the supposed intolerance of stupidity that the presumed epistolary novelist (the letter writer) in fact invents for his subject, the chess player Don Sandalio. This situation, too—seen in the light of our philosophical interpretation of Unamuno's epigraphs—suggests a hidden problem of Idealist orientation, that of whether the letter writer's perceptions or will are sufficient to infer a corresponding reality.

Un pobre hombre rico o el sentimiento cómico de la vida is the fourth Unamuno novel having an epigraph. It is from section V, verse 4 of the Song of Songs and quotes from the Vulgate version of the Bible: "Dilectus meus misit manum suam per foramen, et venter meus intremuit ad tactum eius" (2: 387), the more usual Spanish equivalent being, "Mi amado metió la mano / por el cerrojo de la puerta; / al oírlo, mis entrañas retozaron" (*La Santa Biblia* 793). The intended use is ironic, since the protagonist of the narrative, Emeterio Alonso, is anything but an accomplished seducer. He flees the possibility of a relationship with his landlady's daughter Rosita. After years of bachelorhood, he unknowingly falls in love with the daughter's daughter, but when the girl brings him home he recognizes that he has merely transferred his belated love of the mother to her offspring. This is a repetition of Augusto's bungling use of Rosario as a substitute love object in *Niebla* and Ramiro's crude transference of his frustrated eros for Gertrudis to her sister Rosa in *La tía Tula*. The point in all three cases is that a man may have a healthy sex drive but that it is seriously blunted unless he has the aplomb to put it to use in the right way at the right time. In the case of Emeterio Alonso, the right time arrives later and his presence of mind does not fail him the second time around.

Genette (147) states that the author chosen for quotation is often more important than the epigraph itself. This is not the case with the epigraphs of Unamuno, where the principal thought expressed in the epigraph points only to the idea around which the attached narrative is supposed to cluster. This brings up the question of whether Unamuno uses epigraphs in order to create a locus of meaning when the work itself lacks adequate focus. Only in *Cómo se hace una novela* does the epigraph appear to be used in this way, for the text itself exhibits various competing motifs: autonomy, history as fiction, the creation of a self-imprisoning persona, the farce of the Primo de Rivera dictatorship, and literature as a confluence of intertexts. Despite this singular use of the epigraph to orient a disobedient text, it must be admitted that not even here does Unamuno resort to an epigraph at the conclusion of his work. This unanimous preference for the "introductory" epigraph over the "terminal" one (Genette 149) suggests that Unamuno avoids forcing upon the reader any degree of authorial conclusiveness.

It is important to note that Unamuno quotes all three of his epigraphs accurately. Accuracy is not always a hallmark of Unamuno's quotation. For example, in *Del sentimiento trágico de la vida* and *La agonía del cristianismo* the quotes are often altered or taken out of context so that they may fit Unamuno's own uses. In many articles, Unamuno admits to quoting from memory, and this inevitably leads to some inaccuracies, some doubtless deliberate, since he had one of the keenest and most orderly of memories. We would perhaps expect a higher degree of error in a work arising in a situation of political exile or in that of an equally turbulent post-exile, but such error is not the case with *Cómo se hace una novela*, written in France, or in *San Manuel Bueno, mártir* or *La novela de Don Sandalio*, both of which the author claims to have written in a matter of weeks and which, in any case, were written with Spain in crisis. Genette (54) points out that it sometimes is meaningful to assume that the epigrapher qua fictional entity (as opposed to either the real author of the epigraph or the author of the novel) is the protagonist, for this assumption can give rise to a fuller and more complex reading of the epigraph. For example, if either "Unamuno" or "U. Jugo de la Raza" is seen as the epigrapher of *Cómo se hace una novela*, the epigraph's mention of a "project" or a "problem" suggests the epigrapher's own re-novelizing of life's already intertextualized experiences in the same way that the character of *La peau de chagrin* did while reading the text of his mysterious parchment.

If, on the other hand, we imagine Manuel Bueno to have penned the words quoted from Saint Paul, we are able to see him as imploring the epigraphee to pity him for his inability to believe. If the epigraphee can be imagined as willing to extend him this sympathy, the epigraphee is thereby recast onto the purely diegetic plane, where he parallels

Ángela Carballino—who in a confessional irony, has absolved the priest of his sin of disbelief—and her brother Lázaro—who will become the sympathizing receptacle of most of the disbeliever's most intimate thoughts. If, however, the reader takes Ángela—the novella's true protagonist—to be the epigrapher, the epigraph points up a motif of religious doubt in her that otherwise would continue hidden, and which she may to some extent project in her depiction of the priest. Finally, if we take the "Unamuno" of the work's epilogue as the epigrapher—a very obvious possibility—the doubt falls on "Unamuno" and the real author for whom he voices, and we begin to wonder how much of the priest's disbelief is imposed on him by the obsessions of his authors. In the case of *La novela de Don Sandalio*, equating the epistolary narrator with the act of quoting from Flaubert similarly implores the epigraphee to pity the tragedy of both the writer and his chess-playing subject in their mutual inability to adapt to the ubiquitous stupidity of the world. Indeed, the novel's epilogue—penned by an "Unamuno" suggesting that he might have invented Don Sandalio, the epistolary writer Felipe, and the "lector desconocido" who supposedly passed on Don Sandalio's story to him—implies that a similar pity should be extended to both "Unamuno" and his real-life originator, Unamuno. There is a further deduction to be gleaned from this arrangment. If the epigrapher can be imagined to be a narrator like either the letter writer, his friend Felipe, or the unknown reader who passes on the letters to "Unamuno," the epigraphee becomes equivalent to the novel's narratee, and this narratee could be construed to be a diegetic simulacrum of the actual reader. Therefore, all of the sympathy that the epigrapher implores from the epigraphee becomes the obligation of the "reader." If, however, the epigraph is seen as being addressed to an epigraphee who remains fully intradiegetic and without any association with the real reader, the latter can identfy with the epigraphee only by evolving a sympathetic relationship with the epigraphic text (Genette 156). Given the literary strength of Unamuno's epigraphs, both possibilities function, and the reader is left with the autonomy to read them in either way or in a playful, random manner.

These three Unamunian epigraphs also function to justfy the titles of their works (156). The Augustinian quote about one's life as a preoccupation or project, suggests the "self-making" of the human novel (i.e., life) implicit in the title *Cómo se hace una novela*. The quote from Saint Paul ironically justifies the masochistic "saintliness" of the priest Manuel Bueno, whose surname contributes its own degree of questioning irony. The line from Flaubert that underlines the Flaubertian characters' metabolic incompatibility with human stupidity explains why both Don Sandalio and his narrator will become "jugadores" in a contest to outwit the mediocrity of daily life. Like U. Jugo de la Raza and "Unamuno" in *Cómo se hace una novela*, they will co-create an unclosurable novel that renders their wishes forever possible. Finally, these epigraphs serve to insert their works into a particular discursive tradition (160). The quote from Augustine lends the heterodox treatment of God as both novelizer and novelized in *Cómo se hace una novela* a kind of *erzatz* theological respectability. The Pauline words that initiate *San Manuel Bueno, mártir* give an orthodox ring to the novelist's suggestion that Christ himself may have been a nonbeliever, a suggestion that contradicts and even outdoes Nietzsche's suggestion that the last Christian died on the cross (*The Antichrist* [1888], section 39). The narrator's comment from *Bouvard et Pécuchet* that Unamuno places at the start of *La novela de Don Sandalio* strongly justifies his protagonist's refusal to associate with the kinds of people who lay claim to directing public opinion by virtue of joining an unimaginative social club.

3
Introductions, Prologues, Prefaces

MOST OF UNAMUNO'S NOVELS have introductions, prologues, or prefaces that were clearly written after the author had completed the body of the book, since the introductions comment on the books' central ideas or the completed (completed in the traditional if not the metafictional sense) writing process. The reader, of course, is always free to disagree with the author over the centrality of these ideas or with his explanation of how the book came into being. This disagreement between author and reader is very frequent in the case of the introductions written by Unamuno. For example, the writer's insistence that the parallel between the life of Santa Teresa and that of his character Gertrudis in *La tía Tula* only occurred to him after the novel was written seems doubtful after perusing the six-volume, 1881 edition of her works present in Unamuno's library (Valdés, *An Unamuno* 239) and noting many parallels between the saint's essays and features of his protagonist. His statement in his second edition prologue to *Abel Sánchez* that the book took form as a way of analyzing the blackest part of the Spanish national charcter presents a very dubious epistemology of what is accomplished in that socially de-contextualized narrative.

Porqueras-Mayo (106) fundamentally disagrees with Genette, stating that a prologue does not so much comment on as offer an anticipation of the central text. This view is certainly applicable to *Niebla*, where Víctor debates the character "Unamuno"'s contention that he killed off his own alleged character, Augusto Pérez. Such a comment immediately thrusts the reader into the heart of the narrative prior to reading its first paragraph. The prologues to *San Manuel Bueno, mártir* and, especially, *La novela de Don Sandalio* also do this somewhat, but hardly to the degree of *Niebla*. However, Unamuno's other novelistic prologues, with the exception of "Unamuno"'s post-prologue to *Niebla*, obviously do thrust the reader *in medias res* into the narrative before its formal beginning, carrying out this prolepsis in such a brief and traditional way, that it seems unproductive to stress this ocurrence in examining the paratextual function of prologues in Unamuno's fiction. That is, there appears to be little remaining to be uncovered through an examination of this fleeting phenomenon that might enrich our understanding of his narratives.

Some prologues serve to connect a given work with other works in a series or in an *oeuvre* as well as with an historical period that lends the narrative important dimensions of meaning that would otherwise be lost (Genette 7). We may easily adopt this perspective to observe the inter-work transition present in the fictional Víctor Goti's prologue to *Niebla*, where the prologuist discusses the encounter between *Niebla*'s protagonist, Augusto Pérez, and Avito Carrascal, a character in his previous novel, *Amor y pedagogía*. As Ribbans has shown (87-107), the two narratives develop parallel ideas by recourse to similar characterizations. The same can be said of the prologue-like commentary to Jean Cassou's "Retrato de Unamuno" that precedes *Cómo se hace una novela*, where Unamuno makes it clear that the present narrative explores the same metafictional considerations that arrived at center stage in the final chapters of *Niebla*. The prologue to *Cómo se hace una novela* also underlines the importance of the reader's attempt to identify with the author-protagonist's historical, and not just literary, agony of political exile. It is curious that, in Unamuno's only other novel of historical stamp—the only truly historical (although poetically and not positivistically historical) novel that he wrote—, *Paz en la guerra*, there is no appeal to history, a signal to us that the real significance of its being is to be found elsewhere, as Germán Gullón ("*Paz*" 41-57) has brilliantly made clear.

Some introductions and prologues are directed to everyone and no one, but Unamuno's have in mind a reader intimately familiar with his life and other work but who may be at great chronological remove from him. A good example of this can be found in *Cómo se hace una novela*, where Cassou's "Retrato de Unamuno" envisions a reader knowing little or nothing about the author but where Unamuno's own "Comentario" on Cassou's introductory portrait is anxious to correct Cassou's misleading of a reader that Unamuno had already oriented to his own liking. A salient characteristic of Unamuno's prologues is an insistence upon envisioning a reader picking up his novel decades into the future. It does not occur to him that such a reader may have little interest in the themes he proposes to develop, but he is most aware that each reader will internalize the narrative in a manner dissimilar to his authorly intentions. This is for him the normal relationship of work to reader, and he praises the ability of such a reader to literally re-write his creation to conform to the reader's needs (*Cómo se hace* 140).

Genette (162) tells us that a work may have two prefaces or prologues, one attributed to the author and another to a narrator-character. Such is the case in *Niebla*, where the prologue is attributed to a character, Víctor Goti, who in chapter 17 reveals that he is writing a narrative more or less identical in form to *Niebla*, thus creating a chiastic structure in which each narrative is seen partially as the narrative container and as the narratively contained (Olson, *The Great Chiasmus* 80). The so-called post-prologue to *Niebla*, which follows, and takes issue with statements in the prologue is signed by "Miguel de Unamuno," a character within the narrative. Since 1935, the work has carried an unsigned third prologue, variously titled "Historia de *Niebla*," "Prólogo a la tercera edición," or "Prólogo a esta tercera edición," attributable to the real author. The 1995 edition of Zubizarreta moves this third prologue to a post-texual section titled "Textos complementarios" (Zubizarreta, *Niebla* 287-309). Genette (171) says that a preface may adopt a narrative mode, and this is what happens in Víctor Goti's prologue to *Niebla*. Genette (171) states that the narrative mode is employed when the prologuist is offering an allegedly truthful explanation of how the text was discovered or came to be, and this is in part Víctor's purpose, for he discusses the theories of fiction and humor to which "Unamuno" purportedly wanted to give voice. Genette (179) divides prefaces into two types according to the identity of the sender: authorial prefaces and actorial prefaces, which are written by a character. The second preface or post-prologue to *Niebla*, constitutes the latter type, since "Unamuno" is a character and consequently cannot be Unamuno. Actually, both Víctor's prologue and "Unamuno"'s post-prologue prove to be actorial, and Vauthier goes so far as to recommend that any reader of contemporary narratives assume first that any prologuist is actorial or at least fictitious (*Niebla* 54). The anonymous transcriber's preface to *Nuevo mundo*, the equally anonymous transcriber's prefatory note to *Abel Sánchez* and the "Unamuno"-authored prologue to *La novela de Don Sandalio* likewise offer explanations for the existence of the text and are actorial, but they reside on a hybrid level between the intradiegetic voicings of a narrative character and the even more distant metadiegetic opinions of the real author. Genette distinguishes a subdivision of actorial prologue, the fictive actorial, in which the prologuist functions at the heterodiegetic (first-person, diegetic) level and is additionally a "narrator-hero" (291) of the narrative. Unamuno has no such prologuist. In his only novel possessing a heterodiegetic or even autodiegetic narrator, *Cómo se hace una novela*, the first person prologuist, Unamuno, is clearly distiguishable from the character "Unamuno," who nevertheless continually points to the former. Some might argue that Ángela serves as a fictive actorial prologuist to *San Manuel Bueno, mártir* because hers is also the principal mind through which the priest Manuel Bueno's contradictions must be naturalized, but Ángela's evaluative process is hardly as "heroic" as the struggle of the priest. This discrepancy between the fictive prologuist and the apparent fictive protagonist is to be expected in Unamuno, since most character-prefacers found in world fiction appear attached to autodiegetic texts without fictive actorial prologues. All of these novelistic prologues are ultimately seen to function at the diegetic level, immediately placing in question their authority to comment on the text. Genette (179) also mentions a different classification of preface, the allographic one that is written by neither the author nor a character but by a real-life third party. The only Unamuno novel with an allographic preface is *Cómo se hace una novela*, where Jean Cassou's "Retrato de Unamuno" functions in this manner, offering a view of Unamuno that is markedly different from that offered by the author in his prologue.

It is interesting to note that one Unamuno work that is not being discussed here, the poetry collection *Teresa* (1924), a collection having a lengthy prologue by a novelistic "Unamuno" accounting for the manuscript allegedly authored by a deceased young man, also possesses an allographic preface, this by the long-deceased Rubén Darío. The "preface" has been lifted by Unamuno from a 1909 review of Unamuno's first collection, *Poesías* (1907). It doubtless gave prestige to the newer collection to be "presented" by one who had achieved far greater poetic stature. Indeed, in his prologue to *Niebla*, Víctor Goti paraphrases "Unamuno" and presents in his altered voice an identical theoretical perspective: a neophyte author should be introduced by an already-known one. To a considerable extent, all of the critical (professorial) introductions (necessarily allographic) that have preceded editions of Unamuno's narratives over the past ninety years have also added stature to the author whose work is being thus introduced.

It is also possible for an author to construct a narrative so that one or more of its chapters function metatextually as a preface (Genette 172-73). The just alluded-to chapter 17 and chapters 31-32 of *Niebla* give such a detailed picture of the narrative's structure and metaliterary focus that they can be considered to function as prefaces in the Genettian paradigm. My own view and that of Øveraas (19ff) is that the interior position of these preface-like chapters so surprises the reader that he or she needs to freely reconsider any and all metanarrative clues that may have passed unobserved throughout the majority of the novel. It is therefore difficult to conclude that they produce the same rigidly controlling effect that a prologue or preface usually does.

Prefaces, prologues, and introductions are usually written only after the composition of the narrative text has been completed (Genette 174). This is true of all the prefatory sections of Unamuno's narratives, and almost all of them make this dimension of time absolutely clear. Some prologues and prefaces only appear on the occasion of a second or subsequent edition or at the moment of its inclusion in a collection. Prefatory material may even be added at a much later date, as when a work has been prohibited or its manuscript lost. This is the case with the 1927 prologue to the Spanish-language edition (Buenos Aires) of *Cómo se hace una novela*, a translation carried out by the author himself when the French-language translator and prologuist, Jean Cassou, did not return Unamuno's original Spanish-language manuscript. (Vauthier [Notes to Unamuno, *Manual de quijotismo* 159] disputes Unamuno's suggestion that he could not easily have retrieved the manuscript.) Genette believes that later prefaces are mellower and more reverent than original ones. This is not true in the case of *Cómo se hace una novela*, because Unamuno's growing frustration with the longevity of the Primo de Rivera dictatorship and the length of his own exile infuse its prologuewith a kind of desperation.

Prefacers and prologuists can, from a different perspective, also be divided into real and fictive ones. A real sender has life in the physical world, while a fictive one is purely literary. When a seemingly real prefacer subsequently undergoes an invalidation of his or her physical existence, we witness a transformation of prefacer into an apocryphal being. The first time that the prologuist Víctor Goti appears in the narrative portion of *Niebla* (chapter 3), his status as prologuist is radically downgraded. This also happens when the reader of chapters 13 (the famous "authorial" footnote on *Amor y pedagogía*), 25 (the "author"'s note on his manipulation of his uncomprehending characters) and 31 (the encounter between Augusto and his "author") discovers that the Unamuno of the prologue is really "Unamuno," a character in the novel. (The implied author-prologuist "Unamuno" similarly reveals himself not to be Unamuno when he interrupts one of the narrator-character's letters to Felipe in *La novela de Don Sandalio* [Olson, *The Great Chiasmus* 205].) Genette prefers to call such a prologuist (apparent real author = fictive prologuist) a fictive authorial prologuist (188). The same transformation of a supposedly "real" protagonist into a fictive authorial one occurs when the reader of *Abel Sánchez* begins to suspect, at a completely undeterminable point in the reading process, that the novel's metadiegetic transcriber (author of the prologue-like initial note) may be the protagonist Joaquín Monegro himself. (Franz, *Traces* 45). Genette (186) believes that such a mechanism is most appropriate to an epistolary novel, where the reader initially believes the editor of the text to be the real author. In *Abel Sánchez*, however, we do not have a collection of letters, but a compendium made up of a diary and possible novelistic manuscripts. *La novela de Don Sandalio*, on the other hand, is an epistolary novel. Here the prologuist-transcriber appears to be Unamuno, but in the epilogue the voice of the epiloguist suggests that the prologue may be the work of Felipe—the narratee of the letters—, of the fictionalized Don Sandalio, of the "unknown reader" who passes on the narrative, or of an intradiegetic "Unamuno." In any case, the prologuist falls easily into the broad apocryphal grouping, and his representative assembling and questionable censorship (self-admitted) of the letters calls his authority as prologuist into question. He becomes, in a word, a fictive allographic prologuist (189), one whose final identity as both prologuist and author of the narrative is entirely fictional. While he has no authority as a prologuist, he has infinite authority as the representation of a novelist. This is the central concept of the entire book (as it is in *Niebla* and *Cómo se hace una novela*): all is fiction, and everything imaginable in fiction is authoritative.

Genette (191) tells us that sometimes the real author fluctuates between avowing and eschewing his identity with the prologuist. This is extremely important with regard to the fiction of Unamuno. One of

Unamuno's hallmarks is a constant and most tantalyzing suggestion that his protagonists are himself, and since his prologuists either are himself, someone with ideas similar to his own, someone who humoristically parodies his oft-conceded faults, or someone with the fictional name of "Unamuno" who also appears in the narrative, we may conclude that most of Unamuno's prologues are sufficiently Janus-like to separate the prologuist from the real author and to suggest him at the same time. This fluctuation in perspective is necessary to create the guessing game and sense of play that is so important to Unamuno's ontology of eternity. Ignacio Iturriondo posits that endless peace resides somewhere between struggle and contemplation. Fulgencio Entrambosmares and Apolodoro Carrascal believe in playing a role just enough so that they can freely contradict it. Augusto Pérez outwits and out-authors "Unamuno." Manuel Bueno inspires his parishioners to imbue him with the signs of a faith he really doesn't have and ends up on the verge—but not quite, perhaps in the reader's eye—of being canonized a saint.

Everything in Unamuno's fiction is a game. Everything is open-ended, including the authorship of his prologues. In such a play of prologuist identities, both avowing and rejecting the authorly embrace, it is difficult to decide who is in charge of the prologue, the author or an (to various degrees) autonomous prologuist. This is especially true when we remember that the "author" of both the prologue and the narrative is often only an implied author ("Unamuno"). Morever, a preface or prologue and a postface (a preface that follows, in the language of Genette) can contradict (191-92). When Zubizarreta places the prologue to the 1935 edition at the end of *Niebla*, he makes its account of the post-mortem life of Augusto Pérez contradict "Unamuno's" post-prologue that summarily declares Augusto to be dead. This is a powerful message, coming as it does after the dog Orfeo's epilogue to the effect that Augusto's "novel" of struggle has been eternalized in the animal's thoughts and barks.

Doubtless, prologues and epilogues can contradict as well. The prologue to *La novela de Don Sandalio* states that "Unamuno" has become a recipient of the letters, but the epilogue hints that "Unamuno" or some other diegetic entity may have concocted not only the letters but the entire novelistic apparatus. And who reads the prologue or prologues? This question is unanswerable, but within the narratological embrace of the novel the only possible addressee (often, in Unamuno, a narratee as well) of the prologue is an implied reader. This means that the prologuist must provide a very convincing rhetoric if the real reader is to make the implied reader's imagined reaction his or her own.

The functions of an original prologue and subsequent ones are not necessarily the same. The role of an original prologue or preface is to make sure that the text is properly read. It thus needs to place a high value on the text itself rather than over-valuing the author (197-98). Víctor's prologue to *Niebla* conforms to this dictum, but "Unamuno"'s post-prologue is obsessed with preserving the traditional prerogatives of the author. It is much shorter than Víctor's owing to the transparent egotism that drives it, a situation that would become embarrassingly obvious if the self-defense were permitted to continue. Since Víctor later (chapter 17) claims to be the fictional author of the "nivola" we are reading, his earlier defense of Augusto's autonomy in taking his life (as opposed to "Unamuno"'s authorly claims) is equally self-interested, but the fact that Víctor is defending a third party—a tragically deceased one at that—authorizes a lengthy statement of deference and commiseration.

Unamuno's prologue to *Tres novelas ejemplares* provides a particularly strong orientation to the reading of the text, for it defends the whole Unamunian notion of a dramatic, stripped-down, almost obsessive narrative that is devoid of realist trappings. In it, Unamuno insists that the prologue itself is a fourth exemplary novella, doubtless because it novelistically tracks the author (or "author") in his attempt to give unity to the other three narratives brought under one roof. The atttempt to trace the machinations of the author would soon, of course, become the focus of *Cómo se hace una novela*. In order to make his prologue to *Tres novelas ejemplares* (now titled *Tres novelas ejemplares y un prólogo*) into an alleged fourth novella, Unamuno affixes to its parts the numerals I through VI, indicating that the reader is to approach them as fictional chapters.

Genette notes (201-02) that the function of an original prologue is not only to give formal unity to a disparate text but to provide thematic unity as well. *La tía Tula* offers the best example of a prologue discussing thematic unity, because it places the author squarely behind the importance of exploring and dramatizing women's issues. Almost equally to the point is the prologue to *Cómo se hace una novela*, which centers the reader's attention on the process of intellectualizing the endlessly layered novels of ourselves that we spin out in our search for eternity. It thus addresses both structure and thematics. The prologue to the first edition of *Amor y pedagogía*, however, fails to address the novel's thematic focus because the unnamed fictional prologuist (an Unamuno made "other") spends all his time voicing the imagined public's criticism of the book's stylistic shortcomings and explaining the very real commercial reasons for its large number of paratexts (i.e., its many formalistic configurations beyond its central body). Vauthier (*Arte de escribir* 340) goes so far as to suggest that this prologuist's criticisms/apologies are an attempt on the part of the real author to settle old scores with his critics. Only after the narrative portion of the work is read does it become possible to relate the prologue's terse style and jagged humor to the notion of imposing one's uniqueness on a philosophy of life that is present in the central narrative. This slight reservation about the immediate appropriateness of the prologue to the first edition becomes tempered, however, the minute we examine the actual book published by in Barcelona by Henrich in 1902. Here—as opposed to many later editions, where only slightly wider spaces appear—the cumulative additions to the original prologue are marked by suspension points between the lines. These lines of demarcation clearly offer a foretaste of the agglutinative nature of the ultimate text as a whole. The title of the work helps to set up the narrative's pitting of the improvising individual against the abstract "system." *Niebla*'s prologue likewise accomplishes very little thematic orientation, preferring to concentrate on a definition of Unamunian humor and a justification of humor in a work with metaphysical pretensions. It is only in the reading of the narrative that the reader will connect the prologue's words with the dramatized demonstration in the narrative that the "play" element of the narrative's philosophical humor holds open the door to an unclosured life, possibly an eternal one. In *Abel Sánchez*, the transcriber's note ably (though notoriously incompletely) discusses only the structure of the work. (Discussion of the theme is left for the prologue to the second edition, probably because Unamuno believes that the theme, in this novel above all his other ones, is so obvious.) The prologue written by the transcriber of *Nuevo mundo* offers no orientation whatsoever. The prologue to *Tres novelas ejemplares*, however, points out that its three included novellas—*Dos madres*, *El marqués de Lumbría*, and *Nada menos que todo un hombre*—have a common note of exploring the human will to exist, which, in given circumstances, covers an even deeper will not to exist. Nora, in fact, terms the three novellas attached to the prologue the "trilogía de la voluntad" (García Blanco, Introduction 36). The prologue to *San Manuel Bueno, mártir y tres historias más*, however, by and large fails to unify the inclusion of the 1931 novella *San Manuel Bueno, mártir* with the unpublished *La novela de Don Sandalio, jugador de ajedrez*, and *Una historia de amor*, which the author claims were written earlier and kept in reserve for magazine serialization. (The third novella, *Una historia de amor*, which was added at the last moment and had been published previously, will be discussed later on. It, too, does not fit in with the other narratives.) While interesting for the dating of Unamuno's work and its possible tie-ins to other periods of creativity, most of the prologue is given over to the type of free associations and *non sequiturs* that mar Unamuno's writing when he cannot situate himself adequately within his task. There is, however, a piece of fortunate insight that has been entirely glossed over. After speaking about other's opinions about "mi producción toda novelesca," Unamuno adds, "Y quien dice novelesca—agrego yo—dice folosófica y teológica" (2: 297). In these words of 1933, Unamuno justifies our earlier assertion (see EPI-

GRAPHS) that since the beginning years of his exile Unamuno consciously tended to see his fiction as a dramatization of philosophical questions rather than as exclusively an exploration of the problems of human personality.

One of the novellas included in *San Manuel Bueno mártir y tres historias más*, does, however, contain its own prologue. This is *La novela de don Sandalio*, whose prologue gives pseudo-historical and esthetic orientation, explaining that the letters the compiler has collected about the mysterious life of Don Sandalio were composed in 1910 and are bereft of realistic details. Such information immediately suggests to the reader the skeletal, non-descriptive narratives of Unamuno himself, and the date supplied places the composition of the letters squarely within the period when Unamuno was both most metaliterary and most intent on defying the conventions of realism. This hint of Unamunian meddling in the composition of the letters and perhaps in much more, a suggestion corroborated in the novella's epilogue, recalls another of the collection's included works, *San Manuel Bueno, mártir*, which, while having no formal prologue, contains an introductory paragraph in which the narrator, Ángela Carballino, states that her narrative should be read as a personal confession. Here, too, the epilogue—the word "epílogo" does not appear at the top of the page but is imbedded in the epilogue itself—provides a very different explanation. The epiloguist is no other than an "author" identifiable from his mentioning of *Niebla* as "Unamuno" himself. This "Unamuno" first states that he has changed a few parts of Ángela's text and then admits that he may have written the entire opus. The prologue, where Ángela admits to being a terrible daydreamer, had already suggested a metafictional motif that becomes increasingly obvious throughout the narrative despite most readers' tendencies to forget this focus in favor of a complete identification with the characters. (There is plenty of additional evidence that Ángela's account, despite her professed honesty, may not be completely reliable [Olson, *The Great Chiasmus* 181]). However, at the conclusion of the work, this identification only serves to prove the degree to which collected daydreams (either those of the prologuist or those of the epiloguist) constitute a far more engaging reality than the historical one suggested by the writing of a confession or a biography of an allegedly saintly priest.

Sometimes the unity born of a preface does the work a disservice, since the value of many texts lies in their diversity and unclosurability. Nevertheless, the reading public incessantly exerts pressure on its author to explain what he or she has done (Genette 204). Do any of Unamuno's original prologues excessively circumscribe the reading of their attached narratives? Probably not. Unamuno is acutely aware that plurivalency is the key to his entire metaphysics, and he deliberately sets out to show how each narrative pulls in many directions on multiple diegetic levels. This plurivalency and diegetic separation is what spurs Unamuno to so much free association and dissection of bifurcating word etymologies in his novelistic prologues.

This encouragment of plurivalent readings is not, however a universal hallmark of Unamuno's prologues to subsequent editions. The 1923 prologue to the second edition of *Paz en la guerra*, by exalting the skeletal style of Unamuno's "oviparous" novels, implies that the reader might dispense with his earlier novel's poetry and prolix inheritance from realism, thus unfortunately robbing the reader of much of the narrative's linguistic and historical density or presentation of contradictory motifs. For example, most of the contrasted detailing of the "agonistic" and the "contemplative" Unamuno that Blanco Aguiniaga (56-57) has detailed would be expunged, as would clues to a novelistic sense of the concept of "intrahistory," such as Unamuno detailed it in *En torno al casticismo* (Ribas 71-72). This imaginable result, however, is patently absurd, for as Zambrano clearly shows (Gómez Blesa 13, Zambrano 41, 78), the poetic juxtaposition of apparent *non sequiturs* is the heart of Unamuno's fundamentally "romantic" rhapsodizing of meaning. Even Unamuno's politics is based on an imaginative but always balanced integration of apparently disparate elements (Mezquita 16, 40-41). The first edition of *Paz en la guerra* does, however, contain a unique section that does strongly hint at the type of skeletal or disjointed narrative that would be Unamuno's hallmark beginning with *Amor y pedagogía*. This is the announcement of printing errors ("Advertencia") that, in effect, serves as the prologue to the first edition. After taking responsibility for all of the spelling errors in the book, mistakes he attributes to the "unusual" circumstances of the work's acceptance for publication and first printing, Unamuno provides a composite list of the first instance of an error. However, he adds on the sixth unnumbered page: "Las [equivocaciones] que en la adjunta fe van precedidas de una cruz, son de aquellas [sic] que me atrevo a rogar al lector benévolo que conceda la gracia de irlas corrigiendo sobre el texto mismo, antes de leer la obra" (*Paz en la guerra*, first edition). This necessary involvement of the reader in the co-creation of the narrative will become explicit in the dedication we have already noted to *Amor y pedagogía* and will forevermore be a self-acknowledged constant in Unamuno's subsequent fictional creation.

The 1928, second, edition prologue to *Abel Sánchez* arguably miscasts the focus of the narrative, claiming that it is an allegory of his countrymen's envy rather than that of a human being or all humans. A great deal of universal appeal is lost if one reads these comments narrowly and not as a reaction against those who forced him into exile. The so-titled prologue-epilogue to the second edition of *Amor y pedagogía*, also written in exile, however, clearly orients the reader to all of the play and polyvalency that he or she can expect to find in the narrative. The prologue to *Tres novelas ejemplares* can be viewed as a second prologue to all of its anthologized narratives, since each had been published previously in magazines. In fact, Unamuno specifically points out its much-delayed nature and thereby lays emphasis upon its intended demythologizing of the customary realist practice of seamlessly attaching prologues to the central text (Vauthier, *Niebla* 50-51). Its lengthy discussion of the unfolding ("desdoblamiento") of personality, such as it is displayed in Oliver Wendell Holmes's *The Autocrat of the Breakfast Table* (1906), seriously detours the reader from a "responsible," mimetic reading of these works. It is not only that Juan, Tristán, and Alejandro become different beings—as Augusto Pérez appears to in *Niebla*—when paired with a particular woman, but that the encounter with the feminine "other" reveals them as they really are, someone whom they themselves do not know. This is also the case of Augusto and just about every other important male character of Unamuno.

As mentioned earlier, prefaces may inform the reader of the circumstances under which the work was created. This sort of information seems more typical of a subsequent preface, one that is written after formal and thematic concerns have already been addressed. The preface to the first Spanish-language edition of *Cómo se hace una novela* most visibly jumps the gun in this regard, probably because the book—retranslated and expanded by Unamuno—is already a second edition. The second edition prologue to *Amor y pedagogía* here defrauds our expectations, for it is the prologue to the first edition and its epilogue that explain both how the author's publisher progressively obliged him to lengthen the work and how Unamuno determined to do this paratextually, through the addition of metatexts. The prologue to the third edition of *Niebla* (Unamuno wrote none to the second edition, since the publisher did not inform him of its publication), however, gives a comprehensive view of the ideas that were in Unamuno's head when he set out to write the narrative, and it goes on to show how these same ideas continued to inspire most of his other major narratives as well. It does not, however, discuss personal circumstances, readings, textual modifications, or historical events that might have played a role in the narrative's evolution. This has led to what is, perhaps, one of the greatest areas of speculation in recent Unamuno criticism. Just how did the writer's changing encounters with his circumstance enter into the creative process? Since Unamuno's fiction both before (e.g., *Nuevo mundo* and the early stories) and after the quasi-realistic *Paz en la guerra* downplays the importance of historical setting, it is not surprising that, despite our continuing tendency to marvel at the alleged "uniqueness" of his fiction appearing after 1902, few of his novelistic prologues have anything to say about the material circumstances of each narrative's composition.

Most of Unamuno's prologues, other than the one just discussed, give generous hints about the literary sources of inspiration. These are too many to be addressed here. It must be admitted, however, that in his prologues Unamuno leaves out allusions to the vast majority of his sources. One sometimes suspects that he feels an anxiety of influence when it is a question of what he knows to be his works' more sensational or innovative features. For example, there is no discussion of Galdós's *El amigo Manso* or *Fortunata y Jacinta* in the prologues to *Niebla*, despite our current knowledge that Unamuno based a great deal of *Niebla*'s plot and metaliterary features on those of these two great Galdós narratives (R. Gullón, *Técnicas* 59-89; Franz, *Niebla inexplorada* 17-34). What Unamuno leaves out of the prologues, however, can often be found in the narrative text itself. The latter is frequently rich in concrete references to sources that more often than not blossom into true intertexts. One matter common to prefaces and prologues that Unamuno habitually leaves out is the explanation of enigmatic titles (Genette 213). Why does the title of his third novel juxtapose "amor" and "pedagogía"? Why—in addition to Víctor's inadequate explanation—is *Niebla* subtitled "Nivola"? (The actual narrative is not as spontaneous as the character insists [Pérez 49-73], as we shall remark again shortly.) Just how are the words *Cómo se hace una novela* to be interpreted? There are partial offerings at an explanation, but Unamuno wants the reader to whet his or her curiosity and then read the whole work for an answer. The answer is usually too poetic, too dependent on form, or too involved to be treated in a paratext of any kind.

When a novelist takes part of a prologue to discuss the meaning of a title, it is at times to blunt the public's anticipated criticism of that title or to respond to criticisms offered in the past (Genette 214). Paragraphs 3 and 4 of Víctor's prologue to *Niebla* carry out just such a function, first by stating a certain fear of how the public will respond to the unusual form of the narrative, then by directing the public to Víctor's chapter 17 exchanges with Augusto that specifically define the *nivola*—*Niebla*'s subtitle—that the reader has encountered in the previous 16 chapters. Moreover, these comments are placed in a wide-ranging defense of Unamuno's "oviparous" (spontaneous, post-1897, especially post-1902) novelistic art against criticisms that previous detractors have offered. (Never mind that, since 1914, a host of critics have found *Niebla*'s complexity to be impossible without a great deal of "oviparous" planning [Olson, *The Great Chiasmus* 75-76].) Sinclair has written brilliantly of the ways in which Unamuno's mind alternately advances toward a deeper understanding of itself only to cyclically retreat from what has been discovered (3-4ff), and I myself long ago posited an alternation of oral and written probes in *Del sentimiento trágico de la vida*, with Unamuno first developing a textuality-driven skepticism, then retreating into an oral affirmation of the drive to exist ("Agonía" 395-416, *The Word in the World* passim). Even when Unamuno announces an apparent policy of "no return," he reserves the right to revisit an earlier conviction. "Viviparous" and "oviparous writing, possibility and skepticism, will chaotically achieve dominance at different points of his narrative career.

Genette states that the prologue is often employed to justify the inclusion of a work with a highly innovative form within the customary province of fiction (215). This is the partial purpose of the original prologue to *Amor y pedagogía*, where the unnamed prologuist both voices the presumed public's diagnosis of a "lamentable, lamentablísima equivocación de su autor" (1: 307) and quotes "Unamuno" in his defense against such criticisms. The prologue to *Cómo se hace una novela* provides a subtle justification of its often criticized, crude and "disjointed" form (Nozick 108): "*Una vez escritas, bastante de prisa y febrilmente estas cuartillas* [...] " (*Cómo se hace* 11) is how Unamuno begins his description of the writing process. The prologues to the narrative collections *Tres novelas ejemplares* and *San Manuel Bueno, mártir y tres historias más* rather feebly justify their bringing together (rather ostensibly for commercial purposes) of not inherently related works.

Prologues may also tell the impatient or unqualified reader which difficult sections of the narrative he or she may skip (Genette 218). Víctor's prologue to *Niebla* tacitly tells all unqualified readers to skip the entire narrative if they are not prepared to deal with a humor that will make them vomit all of the ideas they previously have swallowed without thinking about them. He also implies that the unorthodox *nivola* form may not be for them either. The conclusion to section IV of the prologue to *Tres novelas ejemplares* warns the reader familiar with the conventions of realism not to expect the observation of such conventions in any of the included novellas. In an unusual twist on this dispensational function of the prologue, the preface to *La tía Tula* tells the reader that the prologue itself may be skipped!

Some prefaces or prologues are placed after the narrative. For such paratexts Genette coins the word "postface" (237). As mentioned before, Zubizarreta's placing of the prologue to the third edition of *Niebla* after the novel's expository epilogue uttered by the dog creates such a postface. Zubizarreta's decision is a problematic one, for, if by so-doing he restores this paratext to its true condition as an addition written twenty-one years after the novel first appeared, he creates a precedent that he unfortunately contradicts by refusing to place Víctor's prologue and "Unamuno"'s post-prologue—both obviously written after the body of the narative—in the same position. Indeed, the Casa-Museo Unamuno in Salamanca, where the manuscript of *Niebla* is preserved, places and numbers the pages of the prologue and post-prologue *after* the narrative body (Franz, *Niebla inexplorada* 155-66). Unamuno, in fact, frequently admits that his prologues—to both narrative and expository works—are really "postlogues," lamenting that adherence to the custom of explaining something about his fiction in advance seriously devitalizes it. As he states in the prologue to *Tres novelas ejemplares*:

> Este prólogo es posterior a las novelas a que precede y prologa como una gramática es posterior a la lengua que trata de regular y una doctrina moral posterior a los actos de virtud o de vicio que con ella

tratan de explicarse. (2: 192).

In the prologue to *San Manuel Bueno, mártir y tres historias más*, he refuses to offer a narratological explanation for *La novela de Don Sandalio* because "en el epílogo de esa novela he dicho ya cuanto a este respecto había que decir..."(2: 302). Such a statement identifies the contemporaneous performance of the obligatory prologue to the three-work compendium as a veritable "postlogue" to the three included texts. Genette admits that there are very few postfaces or postlogues in literature, arguing that most authors sense that the post-narrative position of the postlogue makes it too awkward and too late to rectify a bad reading of the text (238-39). I am not sure that Unamuno agrees, for the reason that he sees no difference between exposition and narrative. All for him is fundamentally fiction or poetry, and when the postloguist is commenting on the text, he or she becomes a novelistic character wrestling with the same problems of narrative experience that beset the metafictionalizing characters whose ontological identity he or she is trying to explain. He would say the same about the thus fictionalized prologuist and the corresponding ontological (and fictional) identity of the reader.

Later prefaces and prologues are useful because subsequent editions of a book address new readers (239). The preface to the second edition to *Paz en la guerra*, published twenty-six years after the first edition, tries to make readers living much later and in peacetime appreciate the novel's insights born of the second and third Carlist wars (1872-1874) and fortuitously published in 1897, when Spain was on the verge of a disastrous conflict with the United States. The prologue to the second edition of *Amor y pedagogía* (1934) (titled "prólogo-epílogo," because it serves as epilogue to the first edition) acquaints two new generations of readers with the novelist's life (six years of exile) and fiction-writing career (many additional novels) since the publication of the first edition. It also alludes retrospectively to the author's change in novelistic style (at least publically, since *Nuevo mundo* never saw print in Unamuno's lifetime) initiated with the 1902 novel. The third edition (1935) prologue to *Niebla* (1914) represents an almost equal gap and goes over the same recitation of works. It additionally creates a continuation of the saga of Augusto Pérez, the novel's protagonist, in which the character appears to "Unamuno" in a dream and this same "Unamuno" resists the character's beckoning that the "author" bring him to life for a sequel. The irony—not lost on the reader—is that, by writing the new prologue in this way, "Unamuno" (and Unamuno) has already brought him to life, thus anticipating the process of unclosurable continuations later made famous in the bracketed interpolations and progressive additions found in the 1927 (Spanish-language) version of *Cómo se hace una novela*. (It is interesting that, in the post-prologue to the first edition of *Niebla*, "Unamuno" at first seems to be the real Unamuno, but, by the time we read the prologue to the third edition, we know for sure that the prologuist to the first edition was really "Unamuno." For the reader of most recent editions, this occurs even prior to reading the narrative proper, for the third edition prologue usually precedes the narrative text. (If one carefully reads both Víctor's prologue and its reference to his "querido maestro don Fulgencio de Entrambosmares de Alquilón" [1: 476], the eccentric philosopher of *Amor y pedagogía*, and the later reference that the post-prologue of "Unamuno"makes to guidance received from the character Antolín Sánchez Paparrigópulos, one instantaneously grasps the fictitious nature of both of *Niebla*'s prologuists [Vauthier, *Niebla* 49, 60, 74-75].) The preface to the second edition (1928) of *Abel Sánchez*, written in exile, gives a decidedly social interpretation to asocial and ahistorical realities (Marías 156). Here Unamuno states that the envy of Joaquín Monegro is intended as an allegory of the "lepra nacional" (*Abel Sánchez*, ed. Criado, 53) that, in 1924, forced the author himself out of Spain.

Although we have already gone over the prologues to *Tres novelas ejemplares* and *San Manuel Bueno, mártir y tres historias más* as *de facto* second edition prologues to most of the included novellas, it is nevertheless important to add that both prologues offer an esthetic defense of the stripped-down, dramatic style of narrative that most of the anthologized works represent. Why Unamuno feels called upon to do this at such a late date is a mystery. It may be that by, 1920, the date of the first collection, Unamuno had ceased to be associated with many of his previous novels and needed to support his name, early artistic achievements, and revolutionary style anew. We should recall that the publication of *Abel Sánchez* in 1917 was a flop and *La tía Tula* would not appear until 1921. The justification for the skeletal type of narrative that Unamuno included in the prologue to *San Manuel Bueno, mártir y tres historias más* is more understandable. Unamuno had been in exile from 1924 till 1930, and his only intervening novel, *Cómo se hace una novela*, had not yet appeared in Spain. In fact it would not appear again until the late 1960s, when the mutilated version that made it past the Francoist censorship was included in the García Blanco edition of the *Obras Completas*. By 1933, the year *San Manuel Bueno, mártir y tres historias más* was published, Unamuno was sixty-nine years old and nearly an entire Spanish generation was unacquainted with his persona and writing peculiarities. It also needs to be mentioned that the prologue to this 1933 compendium is the only Unamuno prologue that has an appendix. The appendix is necessitated by the last-minute decision of Unamuno to include the final narrative, *Una historia de amor*, which had appeared in *El Cuento Semanal* in 1911 and had never reached a wide audience or a form of display that might lend it greater literary immortality. The appendix is purely pro forma, filled with trivialities, but it communicates two important messages. The first is that the final content of the volume was altered at the very last minute, thus increasing its size and its commercial value. This recalls the way the publisher of *Amor y pedagogía*, thirty-one years earlier, had demanded more and more additions so that the work would bring in bigger profits. The second important message is again that of *Niebla* and *Cómo se hace una novela*: that a good narrative or narrative collection, like a human life, is always making new fiction of itself.

A rather special case that needs to be examined is the "Retrato de Unamuno" by French translator Jean Cassou that follows Unamuno's own prologue to the 1927 edition of *Cómo se hace una novela* but was—that is, Cassou's portrait was—the *de facto* prologue to the original edition of the narrative. This "Retrato," originally a prologue or allographic preface, is demoted to the status of a mere second prologue in the expanded 1927 version. In fact, in the expanded version, it is tightly sandwiched between two very strong texts of Unamuno, a "Prólogo" and a "Comentario." The portrait itself is a rather hyperbolic tribute to Unamuno's strength of personality, fight against tyranny, and existentialist battle to coax a secular faith out of his own mortality. But though such a prologue seems made to order as an accompaniment to *Como se hace*'s histrionic projection of Unamuno's own habitual *agon* with death (Sánchez Barbudo 83-98), Unamuno cannot let it stand, at least cannot appear to let it stand. Therefore, he adds a lengthy "Comentario," which is prelude to all of the bracketed, partially expository additions the 1927 Spanish-language edition of the narrative will add. But far more than illustrating once more the unclosurability of the *nivola* form, the "Comentario" allows Unamuno to effectively rewrite Cassou, not only amending most of what his friend says, but actually intensifying the encomiums through a brilliant display of making Cassou's comments appear limited and trivial compared to his own. This display of combativeness and one-upmanship immediately recalls the scene in chapter 14 of *Abel Sánchez* in which Joaquín Monegro delivers an interpretive speech about Abel Sánchez's painting of Cain, an oration which, through its sheer brilliance, steals the audience's admiration away from the painting and its painter. It can hardly be doubted that this fortuitous intertext, present only due to Unamuno's insistence on writing his ostensibly metaliterary "Comentario," reveals more than any other part of the text the force that drove Unamuno to novelize the process—and the self-imprisonment—of his attempt to make a legend out of this projection of his personal exile. He would use this literaturized persona to wrest from the Spanish dictatorship the public that would otherwise "read" strength into its tyranny's lengthy tenure.

Later prologues never approach a new public without taking into account the reaction of the public that read the earler editions. This previous public usually includes the critic (Genette 240). The prologue to the second edition of *Amor y pedagogía*, written in exile, is directed to a public now far separated from the author, and the latter now alludes to this separation. He asks that the readership realize that his difficult life, particularly the birth and death of two of his children since the original publication date, twenty-six years earlier, have a real-life relationship to the thwarted quest for terrestrial eternity on the part of the novel's character, Apolodoro. Narrative, like life, flows onward or backward—the Unamunian concept of "desnacer"—to results or origins that are uncertain. For its part, the third edition prologue to *Niebla* takes into account the readership of all of Unamuno's previous books and speculates as to why *Niebla* has been translated into the largest number of foreign languages. The answer that the prologuist, "Unamuno," comes up with is that *Niebla* was the most fantastic and tragicomic of his narratives. Few readers would question that *Niebla* is the most fantastic of Unamuno's narratives, but many would find *Abel Sánchez, San Manuel Bueno, mártir*, or all of the novellas included in *Tres novelas ejemplares y un prólogo* equally tragic. (Unamuno admits as much later in this prologue by referring to *Abel Sánchez* as "el más doloroso experimento que haya yo llevado a cabo" [1: 482]). The key to the initial judgment on the part of the prologuist may involve his own frame of mind, having retired from teaching and having witnessed the death of his wife the previous year. The second paragraph of the prologue is completely devoted to the passage of time. Rereading the novel, the prologuist feels old, and he is confident that the readers of the first edition will feel likewise. They may, like he, have become an entirely different person from the one(s) who created or read the book thirty-one years earlier: "Es una obra nueva para mí, como lo será, de seguro, para aquellos de mis lectores que la hayan leído y la vuelvan a leer de nuevo" (1: 478). Yet, Unamuno tells these readers, they can become once more their old selves upon reading the work anew. Through their rereading of *Niebla*, they may also confer a literary eternity on the formerly fifty-year-old author who, in 1914, had written the narrative: "Que me realean al leerla" (479). The prologuist then realizes that a new reading will not be congruent to the original one and that the imagined author thus resuscitated will be different as well: "Pensé un momento si hacerla de nuevo, renovarla; pero sería otra ..." (479). Unamuno is applying to *Niebla* the conclusion at which "Unamuno" arrives in his rereading and expansion of the 1926 text in his production of the 1927 edition of *Cómo se hace una novela*, a discovery that demonstrates that the expanded versions of the 1914 and 1927 narratives, while exploring the same narratological and metaphysical problems, arrive at somewhat different visions of the attempt to create eternity, or even self-deification, through the trick of an unclosurable narrative. Via the 1927 expansion of *Cómo se hace una* novela, Unamuno totally remakes the first version of his narrative. A later Unamuno, doubting the ontological and artistic efficacy of such a feat, hesitates to extend further the already open quality of *Niebla*, a hesitancy from which he had broken loose in his 1927 narrative. Had Unamuno really achieved in either *Niebla* or *Cómo se hace una novela* a personal, hopefully communicable sense of a literaturized eternity? Maybe, but perhaps without preserving the desired degree of personal continuity in the attempted extension and transfer of the experience. The prologue to the third edition of *Niebla* really is not just a prologue but a "metálogo" (1: 484), says "Unamuno." It is a way to have new thoughts about past literary experiences, in the same way that the insertion into *Niebla* of the character Avito Carrascal from *Amor y pedagogía*—he implies in this same prologue—is a means to re-exploring a previously visited ontological problem in a new day. That re-exploration is something less than a conviction of eternity: it is a new onslaught on that quest.

Second edition prologues customarily call attention to corrections or changes made to the text of the first edition (Genette 240). While some of Unamuno's subsequent prologues do mention changes in spelling or punctuation (for example, the prologue to the second edition of *Paz en la guerra*), the more significant of the announced changes involve structural modifications. The prologue to the second edition of *Amor y pedagogía* points out that the lengthy section titled "Apuntes para un tratado de cocotología" that was inserted after the epilogue in the first edition of the novel is not the same expository piece on paper bird-making that he was going to bring out in a French newspaper during the nineteen twenties. (We will take up this paratext of the first edition in the section on EPILOGUES and epilogue-like paratexts.) There is absolutely no bibliographic reason for Unamuno to make this clarification, since the "Apuntes" were part of the earlier edition, where they were attributed to the character Fulgencio Entrambosmares. The "clarification" is a ruse, masking an apparent desire to signal in the intended French article a rewriting and modernization within the "Apuntes," for Unamuno goes on to say: "Las más de las pajaritas que ahora pliego y modelo... no las había inventado cuando plegué esos *Apuntes*" (1: 305). This rewriting and modernization of the twenties' essay is no less than the prelude to the formula for extending *Cómo se hace una novela*. The prologue also rectifies an error in physics that Unamuno has found in one of Apolodoro's internal monologues of the 1902 text. Unamuno goes on to say that he makes this correction as a pedagogue, demonstrating that, although he is the author of a satire on bad pedagogy and incompetent science, he, a one-time aspirant to chairs in mathematics and chemistry, is also capable of bad science. The effect of this observation is to prod the reader into a greater identification with the most human foibles of his tragic, pseudoscientific character, Avito Carrascal.

The prologue to the 1927 edition of *Cómo se hace una novela* explains how and why the "Retrato de Unamuno" by Cassou became part of the first (French-language) edition. What is new to the 1927 edition and is mentioned in the prologue is the "Comentario" and the prologue itself. The significance of the "Comentario" has been discussed above, but the reason for its coming into being appears only in the prologue. It is here that Unamuno discusses how the original Spanish-language manuscript of the work became lost after Cassou had translated it into French and how Unamuno was forced to create the Spanish-language text by translating and adding text to Cassou's translation. This explanation appears necessary for the reader's comprehension of the present volume's form, but no sooner do we arrive at the "Comentario" than we encounter at its conclusion a more specific account of how the original text has been augmented and the observation that the reader will best perceive the narrative's new structure by visualizing its widening spheres of meta-commentaries as a series of Japanese boxes.

Why did Unamuno describe the new textual format in two stages? Seemingly because the prologue and the "Comentario" are on different diegetic levels. The prologue comments on the "Comentario," but the "Comentario" cannot say anything about the prologue because the "Comentario" is actually its compositional antecedent and cannot know the former document. The shorter explanation (that of the prologue) for the 1927 narrative's form is a subsequent commentary upon the more detailed account offered in the previously conceived but later situated "Comentario." It is nearly impossible to believe that the fiery reaction of the "Comentario"—"¡Ay, querido Cassou!, con este retrato me tira usted de la lengua [...]" (35)—was written after the almost scholarly conclusion of the prologue—"*voy a traducir éste* [i.e, Cassou's "Retrato de Unamuno"] *y a comentarlo luego brevemente*" (15). (Zubizarreta states that the prologue was written "a fines de mayo de 1927" and that the "Comentario" took form "*probablemente* entre los meses de mayo a junio de 1927" [Zubizarreta, *Unamuno en su nivola* 23; emphasis mine]. This latter belief is no less conjectural and a good deal less theoretical than our own and flies in the face of our knowledge that the manuscript of *Niebla*, the narrative most similar to *Cómo se hace una novela*, reveals a greatly disordered composition [Franz, *Niebla inexplorada* 155-66]. It also contradicts Zubizarreta's own supposition that Unamuno was very hesitant about the direction that his 1927 additions should take [85-86]).

Why, then, is the metaliterary information in the 1927 prologue and the "Comentario" thus seemingly reordered in the published version of the book? (The actual manuscript and proofs are lost.) Precisely to show that both the bracketed and epilogue material added to the 1927 edition of *Cómo se hace una novela* could just as well have been the starting point for the narrative *had Unamuno chosen to structure things this way*. That is, the innermost Japanese box could be the present additions and the narrative core (the Spanish re-translation of Cassou's 1926 translation) could be the supplement. Such a suggestion sends us back for illustration to *Niebla*, whose overwhelmingly metafictional ending (Øveraas 19-79) must have been glimpsed prior to the slowly mounting crescendo of metafictional suggestions dispersed throughout its first thirty chapters. Admittedly, we could say the same of almost any narrative by any author, and this may be why Unamuno titled his narrative not *Cómo se hace esta novela* but *Cómo se hace una novela*.

Genette (241) notes that a minor function of prologues to second or later editions is to assume authorial responsibility for a text that he or she had originally disavowed. We may consider the 1935 prologue to the third edition of *Niebla* a paratext carrying out just such a function. After suggesting via the prologue and diegesis of the original edition that Víctor Goti may be the author of the work, a very unorthodox work that Víctor terms a *nivola*, Unamuno in the 1935 prologue explains his own compositional strategy and categorically states that "Esta ocurrencia de llamarle nivola… fue otra ingenua zorrería para intrigar a los críticos. Novela y tan novela como cualquiera otra que así sea" (1: 481). Unamuno the novelist-critic thus comes clean professionally about what the novelist has done.

A type of prologue or preface that does not materialize in Unamuno's fiction is the one that Genette terms a "delayed" one. A delayed prologue is usually posthumous or "testamentary" (247). Its primary function is autobiographical, to comment on the author's life and how the work being prologued or prefaced fits into that span of time (248). Almost all of Unamuno's prologues, whether initial or subsequent, do this, and no late ones appear to focus in a particularly conscious way on this objective. A sense of a life as a conscious image about which the author is deeply preoccupied is very unique in figures like Unamuno and Rousseau (Ulmer). It shows how the author, failing to convince him or herself of a religious eschatology, wants to implant a literary one in the mind of the reader. There is scarcely an important narrative of Unamuno's that does not give testimony to this motivation. *Amor y pedagogía* has a dedication to the fictionalized and fictionalizing reader, and, additionally, three characters—Entrambosmares, Menaguti, and finally, Apolodoro—who are obsessed with eternalizing themselves within this reader. *Niebla*'s Augusto tells "Unamuno" that he will live only so long as the "reader" identifies himself with his character. Joaquín Monegro strives to implant his various texts of envy toward Abel Sánchez within both younger generations of his family and the reader who might internalize them. Gertrudis in *La tía Tula* tries to convey her feminist attitudes to younger generations of women, thus perpetuating a persona that hides the insecure and needful self within. The "Unamuno" of *Cómo se hace una novela* maneuvers between the presentation of an honest account of his exile and a dramatized one that is calculated to cast him as a hero. Manuel Bueno inspires a biographer to present him as a saint, thus gaining terrestrial eternity, while successfully hiding from most characters his utter disbelief. A second function of a delayed prologue is to describe the genesis of the text. Again, most of Unamuno's many prologues do this, though not all of his explanations have satisfied and convinced. We have discussed this earlier in the chapter.

Genette (253) points out that delayed prefaces and prologues allow the author to explain how his or her ideas have evolved since the original time of a work's composition. Though Unamuno technically has no delayed preambles, some of the second and third edition prologues written in the last years of his life play this role, and even some prologues written earler (such as the one to the second edition of *Paz en la guerra*, written twenty-six years after the novel's publication) do this. What some of the final years' prologues—those to *San Manuel Bueno, mártir y tres historias más* and the third edition of *Niebla*—do is to highlight one last time their author's commitment to both a process of spontaneous composition and a narrative lacking in social mimetics.

Sometimes a delayed preface gives the author an opportunity to hold forth at length about his favorite works (254). Unamuno, to be sure, does speak about his favorites (*Paz en la guerra*, *Niebla*), lending truth, in the case of the former, to Genette's contention that authors frequently defend on these occasions a work least favored by the public (255). In his repeated praise of *Paz en la guerra* and association of its atmosphere with the memories of his youth in Bilbao, Unamuno also underlines Genette's contention that a delayed or later prologue often inclines toward praising an author's oldest work because it reminds him or her of "the charm of youth and of an innocence or freedom that in later works [he or she] somewhat relinquished" (255). Unamuno, however, does not reserve such favorable comments for a prologue written toward the end of his life. In fact, he often makes such statements in earlier prologues written for relatively unrelated novels he seems less fond of. In some prologues—those written for the second edition of *Amor y pedagogía*, for the third edition of *Niebla*, and for *San Manuel Bueno, mártir y tres historias más*—he seems to reminisce about all of his fiction and point at his movement away from realism after *Paz en la guerra*. There is a certain deception—perhaps even self-deception—in these statements, since *Nuevo mundo* had abandoned realism even before the tardy publication of *Paz en la guerra*, and later narratives—like *Cómo se hace una novela* and, especially, *San Manuel Bueno, mártir* and *La novela de Don Sandalio*—have distinct lyrical qualities associated with their description of nature. It is likely that Unamuno viewed such descriptions, not as realism but as a refinement of the romantic sensibility he had always preserved. Given the neo-romantic attacks on noise, advertising, and the automobile in *La novela de Don Sandalio*, one could perhaps characterize these nature descriptions in *Cómo se hace una novela* and *Don Sandalio* in either way (Schenk 22-27, 163-78).

Delayed or later prologues also tend to emphasize the stability of an author's overall work, stressing his or her "emotional permanence and intellectual continuity" (Genette 256). As we have suggested before, this is particularly true of the prologue to the third edition of *Niebla*. It is also true of the prologues to many other narratives. From *Amor y pedagogía* onward, Unamuno is obsessesed with the contradictions that he and others find in his work. It is as if these contradictions threatened his attempts to lend textual eternity to his personality. From time to time, however, he will exalt such contradictions as signs of his uneradicable vitality. In addition to Entrambosmares's indomitable thoughts in *Amor y pedagogía*, this tendency is most visible in his book *Vida de Don Quijote y Sancho* (1905), in his article "Mi religión" (1911), and in his major essays, *Del sentimiento trágico de la vida* (1912) and *La agonía del cristianismo* (1925).

As said before, the only truly allographic preface/prologue to Unamuno's narratives is the "Retrato de Unamuno" with which the translator Cassou introduced *Cómo se hace una novela*. This separation of sender and text allows the allographic prologuist to praise the text and its author more convincingly than the author or one of his or her characters might (Genette 263-65). Late prologues or prefaces of this type tend to be largely biographical (266), and Cassou's presentation is faithful to the rule. But, since all of Unamuno's own authorial prefaces written during exile are highly biographical, how does Cassou's differ? It is clearly the most filled with encomiums. This, today, makes it perhaps the most suspect, but in its own day, when Unamuno was internationally famous as a type of political prisoner—the exile of a military dictatorship—, it doubtless constituted the most effective type of paratext. Constituting a presentation of Unamuno by a French intellectual to a French intellectual public, it represented the strongest recommendation of Unamuno's intellectual and political credentials. Genette (271) notes that at times the allographic prefacer or prologuist unfortunately disregards the commitments or preferences of the author and simply presents his or her own ideas. Cassou's prologue is of this order, and in his "Comentario" Unamuno disagrees with a great deal of it, partially, as we said, in an apparent effort to outshine his prologuist.

Nevertheless, Cassou's comments on Unamuno's metaphysical struggle with death and the relationship of this struggle to the high profile of the author's political exile are highly relevant, whether Unamuno wants to acknowledge this outside the narrative or not. It seems important to underline that, while the "Unamuno" of the narrative seriously questions whether his exile is a stunt to achieve worldly fame and "immortaliy," the Unamuno of the "Comentario" seems bent on punishing his prologuist for too obviously carrying the fictive admission outside the narrative.

The character Víctor Goti's prologue to *Niebla* represents a bogus allographic document, as do the transcribers' preambles to *Abel Sánchez* and *La novela de Don Sandalio*. Víctor's prologue stands out because it is signed, while the other documents are only later rather clearly tied to an epiloguist or transcriber named "Unamuno." We may say the same thing of Ángela Carballino's opening paragraph of her biography of Manuel Bueno, later titled, presumably by the epiloguist, *San Manuel Bueno, mártir*. In his prologue, Víctor states that he is writing at Unamuno's bequest, since Don Miguel believes that an unknown writer (Víctor) should achieve fame by appending his prologue to the work of an established figure ("Unamuno"). In addition to insulting "Unamuno" by reducing the praise contained in the prologue to the level of an order (here a metacritical one) issued by the "author" (Genette 274), Víctor's performance act is quite the opposite of normal practice where, in a prologue written by a famous personage, "support is usually provided by a writer whose reputation is more firmly established than the author's" (Genette 268). Víctor's own acknowledgment of this situation makes for a theoretical statement that entirely contradicts that of Genette:

> Parecerá acaso extraño a algunos de nuestros lectores que sea yo, un perfecto desconocido en la república de las letras españolas, quien prologue un libro de don Miguel, que es ya ventajosamenteconocido en ella [...] . Pero es que nos hemos puesto de acuerdo don Miguel

y yo para alterar esta perniciosa costumbre, invirtiendo los términos, y que sea el desconicido el que al conocido presente. (1: 469)

Once more, the order in which apposite documents (here the prologue actually written to present "Unamuno" and the other one that could have been developed to present Víctor, the latter a function carried out only in a begrudgingly inferior manner through "Unamuno"'s post-prologue) appear largely irrelevant and open to alteration. The important thing is to make a statement about the infinite alterability of life and the text, so that all metaphysical and eschatological possibilities are held open.

In *Niebla*, Víctor's paratext constitutes not only an allographic prologue, but an allographic actorial one, because he combines the role of an outside party with that of a character (Genette 276). "Unamuno"'s comments in the post-prologue are equally actorial and decidedly more allographic owing to the undeniable suggestion that "Unamuno" is to a great extent an imitation of the historical Unamuno. "Unamuno," being both actorial and allographic, carries out the function of correcting "in a straightforward way, a few errors of fact or interpretation" (276) voiced in Víctor's prologue. However, the actorial dimension of "Unamuno," discovered only during the reading of the final chapters of the narrative, militates against the reader giving "Unamuno" the degree of interpretive authority that he demands. The "Unamuno" of the prologue to the third edition, who writes of the dream in which Augusto appeared to him and demanded a continued existence, is equally actorial and has equally diminished authority. Although the name "Unamuno" suggests an association with the historical Unamuno, the fact that the two are not synonymous serves to distance the prologuist's words from those of Unamuno (Genette 279). The real Unamuno would not argue with his character, but the fictional "Unamuno" would, in the same way that "Carlyle" disputes with his characters in *Sartor Resartus* and his *History of the French Revolution*, both of which Unamuno had translated. Indeed, in Unamuno's many comments on Carlyle's *Life of*

Oliver Cromwell that were issued over the years, a second-level diegetic "Unamuno" hectors "Carlyle" as the latter argues with his characters.

In order to make a fictional prologue appear to be real, the prologuist must flesh it out with many details culled from the historical reality of the author whose work is being prologued. In other words, the fictional prologue must parody the real author's work and anchor itself, so to speak, in that author's reality (Genette 279). The fictional transcribers' statements at the beginning of *Nuevo mundo*, *Abel Sánchez*, and *La novela de Don Sandalio* parody the serious writing of criticism and history and thus take on some of the serious intent of the genres being parodied. The transcriber's statements at the conclusion of *San Manuel Bueno, mártir* do this too, but in this case the author has chosen to include the metatextual comments in the form of an epliogue rather than as prologue. However, the brief prologue-like paragraph written by Ángela that is inserted into the first page of *San Manuel Bueno, mártir* also gains verisimilitude by parodying the methodology of a biographer, though in this case it is immediately coupled to the visionary proclivities of a novelist. In three of these cases, the writer of the text accounts for his or her ability to offer writing appearing originally as a diary (*Nuevo mundo*), autobiography (large parts, perhaps even all of *Abel Sánchez*), or correspondence (*Don Sandalio*), thus lending a further illusion of substantiality to the characters and incidents described.

A very different function of a fictional allographic prologue is to permit the author to disavow the statements expressed therein (Genette 282). The prologues to the first edition of *Amor y pedagogía* and *Niebla* respectively offered by an anonymous prologuist or by Víctor Goti do this to create a (temporarily) believable base from which to launch criticisms of Unamuno's and "Unamuno"'s art of the novel. This base must be believable because the author of both works ultimately wishes his allegory to launch a plurality of possible interpretations not only of the fictional world but of the phenomenic one as well. However, the fact that the prologuist is fictional immediately erases the generic distinction between fiction, on the one hand, and theoretical or explicitly philosophical content, on the other. This is true both of simulated allographic prologues (ones that are parodic but not attributable to a character) and fictional allographic ones like those we have been discussing here. As Genette observes, most fictional prefaces mirror the narrative text's own metatextual operations and thus underline the self-consciousness of the work as a whole (292). But this unanimity of function does not necessarily mean that the blurring of the diegetical plane merely eases the admission of metatextual commentaries into the prologue. It also makes the prologue and the narrative it is appended to appear to be real and not merely fictive (288). When an a fictive allographic text is coupled to a text that also is fiction, the product paradoxically turns out to be a sense of reality, because the "real" reality is thereby eliminated. Therefore, to sum up, fictional allographic prologues tip themselves and their attached narratives both toward the outside world and toward the inner, idealistic world of fiction, a paradoxical situation productive of the type of open, Kierkegaardian dialectic that favors an Unamunian metaphysics of perennial possibility. If this seems ontologically purposeless, we need to remember with Olson that "it is really only in terms of a rationalistic logic that Unamuno's dialectic fails to find 'synthesis'" (*The Great Chiasmus* 4). It is doubtful that Unamuno does all of this in a way that is entirely conscious. It is a product of his whole metabolic and philosophical predispostion, one that LaRubia (*Alegorías de la voluntad*) everywhere terms "orgánica."

4
Notes

GENETTE'S DEFINITION OF A note is "a statement of variable length [...] connected to a more or less definite segment of text and either placed opposite or keyed to this segment" (319). Though a note appears very different from a prologue or preface, it has in reality a similar function: both offer a commentary on the narrative text (320). The Unamuno narrative having the most conspicuous notes is *Niebla*, where, in chapter 13 "Unamuno" places a footnote identifying Apolodoro Carrascal as a character already having appeared in *Amor y pedagogía*, and in chapter 25, where this same "Unamuno" inserts an internal note to inform the reader that, while Augusto and Víctor appear to be engaged in an intense dialogue, they are not real people but characters in a novel that he is writing. The bracketed insertions of text in the 1927 edition of *Cómo se hace una novela* also might be considered notes, since one of their functions is to comment on the original text of the 1926 edition. Genette states that, when the sender of the note is actorial (is an actual character in the central corpus), the note adds or contributes to the "biography" of the person who is its subject (322). This is an accurate statement of what occurs in both of these Unamuno narratives, for the note in *Niebla* reveals the diabolical self-confidence of "Unamuno" that will later (chapter 31) be his temporary downfall at the hands of his character Augusto, while the notes in *Cómo se hace una novela* underline the tragic dialogy of "Unamuno," a protagonist who wants to be free and honest but whose desire to create a heroic persona prods him to control the explicitly inscribed "reader"'s appropriation of the original text. This motivational and structural chiasmus can only point in the direction of an unclosurable situation, as De Kock (128-29) clearly points out in his study of Unamuno's *Cancionero* (1953). In the cases of both "Unamunos," the openness of the narrative text ultimately saves each of these actorial note senders (and their "reader") from the deadly univalency of their intended writerly control. The note sender and the "reader" (also, hopefully, the real reader) are thus free to follow any mixture of narrative threads that will aid their hope for survival via their internalization of the characters' existential plight.

There is another Unamuno work that possesses notes. It is the poetic collection *Teresa*, which we have discussed in a previous section despite its falling somewhat outside our focus on paratexts surrounding and imbedded in narratives. Both here as well as in our previous discussion, our justification is grounded in the many narrative techniques and prose segments visible in the collection (González López 84-89). In *Teresa*, the prologuist-transcriber presents a collection of poems honoring his beloved that Rafael, a poet dying of frustrated love and tuberculosis, has bequeathed him. In the notes, which are extremely lengthy and numbered I-XII, "Unamuno" gives copious hints (as he does in the prologue) that he and not the fictitious "Rafael" is the true author of the poems. The use of such endnotes implies scholarship and and thus a quest for clarity, but the effect of the notes is to make the attribution of the text to an alleged author ambiguous. Are we to understand that the author of the poems is "Unamuno"? Or is the "Unamuno" of the prologue and notes merely positing his own real writer, Unamuno— who perhaps only invents "Unamuno," "Teresa," and "Rafael" in order to construct a modern allegory of the creation of the equally posthumous *Rimas* of Gustavo Adolfo Bécquer—as the author of the poems? Each choice has its merits, and a superimposition of all three possibilities—Rafael, "Unamuno," and Unamuno—produces a prolixity of interpretive possibilities that again casts the inscribed "reader" (and the reader) in the role of the author and underlines his/her own freedom (should he or she want to avail themselves of it) to see only openness where the text of the poems presents an indecisive dialogy of hope and despair.

Genette elaborates five specific types of notes: (1) authorial notes to an authorial text; (2) authorial notes to a narratorial text; (3) authorial notes to an actorial text; (4) pseudo-editorial notes to an actorial text; and (5) notes that are attributable to more than one sender (323). *Niebla*, to pursue only one example, exhibits all of these possibilities. One may consider the historical Unamuno to be the author of the chapter 13 and chapter 25 notes and judge the entire narrative to be his work. One may also see Unamuno to be the author of a metatextual note, the note in chapter 25, appended to a narrative related by an unspecified narrator. It is likewise possible to see both notes as a fictional artifice affixed to a narrative written by a character-author like Víctor Goti. Finally, the note may simultaneously be attributed to all of these. Genette's list, however, does not exhaust *Niebla*'s possibilities. The note may be an instance of what the "reader" (or reader) has all along been thinking. It may be the work of Augusto, who has been able to project the "nivola" of his life onto his writerly friend Víctor (as he implies he will in chapter 31) and in the projection has decided to step back and comment on himself as "other." It may in part be an imposition of the metatextual tradition implied in the narrative's many intertexts and explicit references to Cervantes. We are free to mix these perspectives at will and to deduce from them a lesson about the orderly multivalency of the universe that may be applicable to our own dreams for perpetuity.

To whom are Unamuno's novelistic notes written? One immediately assumes that, in the case of *Niebla*, they are addressed to the real reader of the text, but the prologue's, the post-prologue's and the central narrative's references to an inscribed "reader"—in other words, a narratee, though not always one on an identical diegetic level—open myriad interpretive possibilities. In *La novela de Don Sandalio*, the note inserted at the midpoint of chapter 15 is clearly addressed to a narratee, but that narratee is never inscribed into the central text but into another paratext, the novella's epilogue. This situation, unlike that of *Niebla*, keeps the real reader outside the novel's hermeunetics until he or she succeeds in identifying with the narratee as an exemplar of the real reader's situation. Genette (324) points out that not all individuals would be prospective readers for every type of note. The note in chapter 25 of *Niebla* would appeal only to a reader capable of following the narrative's commitment to play and a mapping of narratological structures. The bracketed notes to *Cómo se hace una novela* fail to annoy only a reader interested in the life of the exiled Unamuno or capable of perceiving the autogeneration of narrative implied by the juxtapositon of the 1926 and 1927 texts. The laborious endnotes to *Teresa* require a reader both accustomed to literary scholarship and prepared to recognize its parody ultimately put to a serious purpose.

Sometimes notes to works of fiction are totally discursive, marring for many readers the narrative mode of the work itself. We might think of the the digressive notes to the reader in Sterne's *Tristram Shandy* (1759) or—though they are paratextually another matter—the discursive passages and the first of the two epilogues with which Tolstoy delays the reader before a final resolution—in the second of the post-narrative additions—of the lives developed in *War and Peace* (1865). In Spain, the "Paralipómonos" section of Valera's *Pepita Jiménez* (1874) has internal notes, and Pérez de Ayala's *A.M.D.G.* (1910) has many explanatory footnotes. Such discursive notes customarily adorn narratives, Genette tells us, that were already generically "impure," ones that mix fictional attributes with large doses of philosophical or metaliterary reflection (332). It goes without saying that Genette's statement applies perfectly to all of the major narratives of Unamuno, an author who has come to be considered, almost *malgré lui*, a theorist and philosopher—this despite the far greater popularity of his fiction—and who always insisted on the folly of separating fields and genres. Authorial notes, which originated in the physical, medical, and social sciences, seem increasingly "transgressive" the more a narrative gets away from a focus on history (Genette 335). *Paz en la guerra* would be the perfect place for a note, but the novel has none. *Niebla* seems a particularly improbable location, as the work is deliberately isolated, at least in appearance, from the events of the real world. In fact, however, the work includes many economic factors and class conflicts that are not apparent in a first reading (Franz, *Niebla inexplorada* 49-76, 113-24), and Víctor's discussion of a sonnet by Manuel Machado and the mentioning of his brother Antonio in chapter 17 indicate (along with the 1914 date of publication) that the narrative action transpires during the first years of the twentieth century, a fact which provides a background for the interpretation of certain facets of character behavior. Nevertheless, Unamuno deliberately excluded the appearance of a social novel, doubtless so that the details would be thin enough for the reader to distinguish the narrative's philosophical and metafictional motifs. *Cómo se hace una novela* is an historical hybrid. The story of U. Jugo de la Raza that the 1926 version presents is largely a-historical and asocial, however, the metatextual narrative of "Unamuno" writing La Raza's story is infused with a great deal of the real Unamuno's exile. The 1927 version, with its interior additions and final continuations, becomes overwhelmingly historical. A change in this direction is already visible toward the middle of the primitive version (Zubizarreta, *Unamuno en su nivola* 74-75). *Teresa*—even its strictly narrative portions—is not historical at all, yet it is overwhelmed with quasi-historical notes.

It appears from all of this that Unamuno deliberately transgresses generic conventions to insert notes where they are least expected, and, if there is no justification whatsoever, he will transform the narrative into a history in order to playfully rationalize the note he has inserted. *De Fuerteventura a París* (1925), another hybrid work mixing poetry and prose, ahistoricity and historicity, is a case in point. Unamuno doubtless began to write a work of poetry entirely comprised of political sonnets in the spirit of Quevedo and Carducci. Until the end, he stays within the strictures of meter and rhyme, at times limiting himself to an allegorical expression that removes the appearance of history. But as the poems progress, none-too-subtle historical and political references overpower the expression, producing an ebb and flow of lyricism amid crescendos of bitterness toward those held responsible for his exile. Finally, Unamuno seems to realize that the original form and lyricism may be an impediment to an expression of the historical moment, and he inserts a massive series of prose explanations (glosses or notes if you will) that explain the historical origins and symbolism of the poems. (It is necessary here to point out that, in an aside, Genette finds the origin of the entire paratext of the note in the medieval phenomenon of the marginal gloss [320], an explanation that draws the many discursive additions to *Cómo se hace una novela* even more firmly into the realm of the note.) Is *De Fuerteventura a París* a work of poetry, with all of the polyphony that the word poetry implies, or is it a work of narrower focus, of ideology? Has it become a work of fictionalized biography with the poems rendered supplementary to the recounting of history? The work's subtitle, *Diario íntimo de confinamiento y destierro vertido en sonetos*, suggests both perspectives and refuses to divulge any authorial preference. It is the addition of the notes, however, that creates the distinct *illusion* that even the poems have their roots solidly in history. But this statement cannot be our final judgment because the note is, by tradition, supplementary and always *suggests* that the entity responsible for the note knows less than the entity responsible for the poem or narrative (Genette 335). The somewhat difficult-to-identify author of the notes to *Niebla* and the "Unamuno" who added the notes to *Cómo se hace una novela* presumably know less than the historical author, but the historical author, via the narrative itself, has been allegorically reduced to the status of his characters' puppet. We are left suspended to ponder.

A note can mark a break or change in the flow of a text. It can signal a "fork in the narrative [...] in a work which at each juncture would show the diversity of solutions that can present themselves to the mind [...] " (Genette 335-36). Øveraas (14-15) has shown how the footnote referring to *Amor y pedagogía* inserted into chapter 13 of *Niebla* marks the formal transition from the mostly mimetic "texto de Augusto" to the concentrated, metafictional "texto de Unamuno" in the final chapters of the narrative. The longer note in chapter 25 only confirms the transition. Allographic notes are usually editorial notes (Genette 337), and one can scarcely read an Unamuno narrative today without finding in the edition a collection of scholarly notes. Most of these deal with the identification of allusions to literary and philosophical texts or to the few historical personages mentioned in the narrative. A perusal of *Niebla*'s many editions shows a great deal of agreement about the manuscript and the approximate time that Unamuno completed his first draft but comparatively little harmony in interpreting or even counting the many interpolated novellas (Jurkevich, "Unamuno's" 3-14). There has not been unanimous agreement about whether to include the 1935 prologue to the third edition as part of the text, nor whether to place it at the beginning or at the end of the narrative. Most surprisingly, there is no unanimity in the choice to include or exclude from the title page the phrase—present in the first edition—"Prólogo de Víctor Goti," which presents the illusion of an historical allographic prologuist that is destroyed in both the prologue and "Unamuno"'s post-prologue.

Some editorial notes are only pseudo-editorial notes, in actuality attributable to an actorial "author" or another character. Although the notes to the semi-fictional *Teresa* fall into this category, the only Unamuno works traditionally classified as a narrative that adhere to this formula are *Niebla* and *La novela de Don Sandalio*. What is unsettling about this type of pseudo-authorial practice is its destabilizing of authority over the state and presentation of the text. It is not only that the authority passes to a fictional character but that, in some instances, the character, too, is an author (Genette 339). In *Niebla*, *Don Sandalio*, and *Teresa*, this charcter is no other than the novelist-poet "Unamuno." The reader presumes that outside this "Unamuno" stands a look-alike historical author named Unamuno and that, beyond Unamuno, there exist an infinite variety of "Unamunos" in the mind of the books' readers. This *mise-en-abyme* creates a situation in which authority is forever differed. Like the famous paradox attributed to the skeptic philosopher Zeno, in which distances are forever halved without ever arriving at a destination, authority never comes to rest on anyone, and consequently everyone is free to concoct his or her own overlay of attributions. This situation may fit in well with Unamuno's practice of manufacturing metaphysical optimism out of infinite play, but it also reminds one of the psychologist's judgment that a child, left without a clear structure of parental authority, will react with terror when abandoned to face apparent chaos.

5
Epilogues

GENETTE DOES NOT CONSIDER epilogues to be paratextual, doubtless because they are in most instances a continuation of the narrative text. Unamuno's epilogues are a special case because either they do not continue the text or they clearly perform other functions that are not narrative. In only four narratives, *Amor y pedagogía, Niebla, San Manuel Bueno, mártir* and *La novela de Don Sandalio,* is the word "epilogue" used, and in each of these situations the added material is more metatextual than narrative. This appears to be an extension of Unamuno's overall tendency to use epilogues or addendum-like structures in his construction of tropes and enthymemes. That is, they represent a part of the central text's logic that has heretofore remained absent, constituting the synechdoche of a counter-world that unclosures the original conclusion. Olson (*The Great Chiasmus* 16-17, 196-97), for example, finds such addenda to be one of the techniques Unamuno uses to make his frequent employment of linguistic and narrative chiasma appear open-ended despite the contrary pull of many chiastic structures.

The manuscript of the early, though posthumously published, *Nuevo mundo* that Laureano Robles has assembled possesses a post-narrative addition titled "Notas para *Nuevo Mundo*" (77-84) that the author, thinks Robles, at some undeterminable point considered adding to the text and which may be more of an epilogue than a series of notes. But if the "Notas" are an epilogue, they are indeed a strange variety, for, after a brief note-like section by the fictional "transcriber," they present isolated "documents" that take the deceased Eugenio Rodero's life back to an earlier moment in his native village, that is, before the Madrid episodes that constitute the narrative body of the work. Tanganelli ("Introduzione" 12) theorizes that the "Notas" record part of an early draft of the novel, including the insertion of a new section that appears later, outside *Nuevo mundo*, as the independently published (1898) story"Beatriz," a theory that is credible, given Tanganelli's evidence that the "Notas'T and "Beatriz"stylistically and thematically conform not only to one another but to other fragments that Unamuno stored with them, namely an untitled piece that the novel's first scholarly editor, Laureano Robles, has titled ["Gabriel"], and another piece that Unamuno provisionally titled "El fin de un anarquista" (Tanganelli, "Introduzione" 14-16). One may question both, however, whether Unamuno's decision to exclude these fragments can be considered definite and whether his retention of the fragments within the same envelope containing the manuscript of *Nuevo mundo* does not hint at a future intent to insert them at a point much later in the text than the original (but rejected) one suggested by Tanganelli. (Evidence suggests that Unamuno frequently shuffled folios as he rewrote *Niebla* [Franz, *Niebla inexplorada* 155-66].) There is only one Unamuno narrative that actually involves lengthy and consistent analepses like the one we posit here, namely *Abel Sánchez*, a novel whose internal, autobiographical *Confesión* often returns to earlier stages in Joaquín's life. If we use *Abel Sánchez* as a guide to what Unamuno might have had had in mind in *Nuevo mundo*, we are confronted with a paratext that is intended to be as much a retrospective insertion as an epilogue. It is an insertion that, beginning at a diachronically much earlier moment, subsequently follows Rodero from the moment that he falls ill in Madrid to the instant of his death. This is a death that had been summarily mentioned (*Nuevo mundo* 64) just prior to the sample expository text culled from Rodero's philosophical speculations that concludes the narrative nucleus of the work. The intended effect of the epilogue's addition is apparently to render in more complete fashion what was left in an incomplete and unsatisfactory form in the original version, but as Tanganelli—who, we repeat, posits a compositional explanation much more conservative than our own—adds, its potential effect is to transform the narrative from a mini-biography of Eugenio Rodero into a poetic (and therefore synchronic) evocation of what would later become Unamuno's christological and almost mystical essay, the *Tratado del amor de Dios* ("Introduzione" 13). In actuality, on the metafictional level, the definitive epilogue to this particular narrative does not take form until thirty years later, in the original version of *Cómo se hace una novela*, where Rodero, now called U. Jugo de la Raza, falls ill and prepares to face death upon reading the words predicting the death of any reader who finishes Balzac's *La peau de chagrin*. In this latter version, Unamuno does not let his character die because the latter keeps deferring the reading of the final, fatal pages of Balzac's book. This is precisely what Unamuno may have been planning to do with *Nuevo mundo*. Robles (77-101) has appended to the original manuscript of the novel three related but separate texts—a series of philosophical fragments; a story that Robles, as we pointed out earlier, has speculatively titled ["Gabriel"]; and a narrative fragment titled "Eugenio"—that appear to indicate a desire to prolong Rodero's fated existence with continuations and insertions that will narratively reproduce the non-movement, and therefore the non-conclusion, theorized in the—for Unamuno—hopeful paradox of the Sophist, Zeno, who schemed to do away with time.

Amor y pedagogía has more than one epilogue. The first, formally titled "Epílogo" presents an admixture of metatextual comments, additions to the narrative's plot, and an explanation of how the editor Valentí Camp had reiterated the need for a longer version of the novel if the Henrich publishing house was to accept the text for publication. It is a true epilogue, though an unorthodox one that playfully combines genres and demonstrates the ability of the inscribed "author" to both prolong his text and rhapsodize an optimistic conclusion to the story. But there is still another epilogue, a section titled "Apuntes para un tratado de cocotología" that in the narrative is attributed to the somewhat pedantic character Fulgencio Entrambosmares. The transition to the "Apuntes" is carried out via the device of an "authorial" statement in the first epilogue to the effect that the publisher has asked the "author" for added text, and he has received it from the obliging Entrambosmares. Vauthier (*Arte de escribir* 336) correctly points out that the diegetic implied author, "Unamuno," here actually depends on the equally fictional Entrambosmares's help in order to enlarge the narrative to the size stipulated by the real editor Valentí Camp. Here in this second epilogue, however, the pathetic, existential dimension of the original character, Entrambosmares, is lost, apparently to concentrate on a, today, not very humorous parody of Unamuno's former teacher, Marcelino Ménendez Pelayo (Vauthier, "Epistolario" 108) and a number of the more seminal philosophical influences on Unamuno, now found to be of limited value to him (Franz, "The Philosophical Bases" 443-51; Olson, *The Great Chiasmus* 57). It is not in the "Apuntes"'s explanations of origami that we find the epilogue function carried out, but in the philosophical comments that justify particular folds in the paper that are necessary to produce the birds. One suspects that the justification *ex post facto* of the actual folds in the paper represents a sarcastic comment on reason applied to the vitality of inspiration. It is hardly stretching matters to say that the "Tratado" constitutes an implicit defense of the "viviparous" compositional process and *nivola* form that subtend all of *Amor y pedagogía*.

There is, however more. The second edition of the novel has a third epilogue titled simply "Apéndice" that, in a third-person "authorial" voice, supplemented by a lengthy text from Entrambosmares himself, presents both information about the philosopher's life over the thirty year period since publication of the first edition and further observations on the theory behind the act of paper bird-making. The inclusion of drawings and comments about the symbol of the swastika direct the contemporaneous reader to a comparison between the deadly plans of the character Avito Carrascal to create a genius and the even more tragic ideas of Hitler to produce a master race. The addition of this much delayed epilogue demonstrates that theories such as Carrascal's are "intrahistoric," constituting a divisive, self-destructive human predisposition that must forever be guarded against. At the conclusion of his "Apéndice," "Unamuno" reveals that he might be tempted to write further appendices but that then the work would suffer from "appendicitis." Olson finds that, coupled to the novel's prologues, this string of epilogues has the effect of sandwiching the narrative body between them, thus producing an open-ended chiasmus in which the narrative is always becoming exposition and the exposition is becoming narrative (*The Great Chiasmus* 58).

Niebla's epilogue is justly famous. It is the "Oración fúnebre" (its subtitle reads "Por modo de epílogo," all in capitals and in large type in the first edition, so as to emphasize its originator as proto-"writer" rather than as mere happenstance eulogist) expressed largely (with an introduction in the voice of the narrator) by Augusto's dog Orfeo upon the death of his master. One wonders (since the manuscript itself yields no firm evidence) how long after the creation of the narrative body Unamuno decided to add this section, because it refers incorrectly (Edelmira) to Eugenia's aunt (Ermelinda). (Edelmira was the wife of Entrambosmares in *Amor y pedagogía*.) The final chapter of the narrative had ended with a sentence that gave more than satisfactory closures, those of death and *denouement*—to the entire amorous saga of Augusto: "Y aquí está la historia de Augusto Pérez" (1: 666). In the epilogue, Orfeo reveals that, to him, the deceased Augusto was like a god, though a rather incomprehensible and at times a stupid one. This characterization more or less parallels Augusto's perception of "Unamuno" in their famous encounter of chapter 31, and both characterizations presumably apply to the God in whom the real author rather publicly and melodramatically tries to believe outside the narrative. (In his prologue, Víctor Goti reports that "Unamuno" has justified the practice of other authors who make sport of God [1: 474].) Just as Augusto, abandoned by "God" (his author), seemingly has disappeared into the "niebla" of whatever follows death, Orfeo, now without Augusto, feels incapable of keeping his Augusto-mirrored existence together. With the death of his "other," Orfeo must die too. Therefore the next day Augusto's housekeepers find Orfeo dead. This situation does not merely serve to underline some metaphysical and metacritical concepts—the need for the "other," God's dependence on his creatures, and the author's creation of his characters in order to plant his own existence in the reader—already visible in the narrative, but also to reintroduce the note of creative playfulness upon which Víctor and his "nivola" predicate that the hope for eternal life may depend. If dogs can talk about metaphysics, there is a good deal about life's possibilities that we have not yet discovered.

Abel Sánchez, La tía Tula, and the three novellas (four if we obey the prologuist and count the prologue itself) in *Tres novelas ejemplares y un prólogo* have no epilogue if one applies the usual definition. (On the technicality that it comes at the very end of *Abel Sánchez* and is printed in capitals, someone might argue that the exclamation "¡QUEDA ESCRITO!" [791] contributes a type of epilogue attributable to either Joaquín [if one is willing to grant him authorship of the entire work], the unnamed presenter of the text, or an unlabeled "Unamuno" who alludes proleptically to the "Unamuno" who in 1928 will pen the prologue to the second edition, where the agonizing experience of writing the work is mentioned. If the latter, we have an addition that, late in the novel, introduces the same sort of revelation of authorial control that we have in the various notes [see previous chapter] inserted by "Unamuno" throughout *Niebla*. Or, one might choose to consider the exclamation another note.) *Cómo se hace una novela* has its 1927 continuation, which is a legitimate epilogue in the same way that the bracketed insertions constitute legitimate glosses or notes on the surrounding, previously published text. The continuation of the story of "Unamuno"'s exile demonstrates that a character (in the game of fiction, supposedly also a human) can step outside his author- (i.e., God-) prescribed role and achieve an unexpected endurance. It also shows how an "author," "Unamuno," takes pity on the plight of his own creature, U. Jugo de la Raza, and determines to devise a way to save him before he is devoured by his reading of Balzac's deadly text. If "Unamuno" can take such pity on his character within an allegory, God—in whose own image "Unamuno" was made—can, in turn, take pity on Unamuno and the reader. This is a successful analogy groped for but never achieved in the final chapters and epilogue of *Niebla*. But Unamuno is not content to let his characters' odysseys conclude on an analogy. After provisionally concluding the continuation, on 17 June, 1927, with the admonition that every reader must make himself a co-creator and co-creature of every narrative, he turns around and appends seven more—this time carefully-dated—continuations of the narrative. He has rescued U. Jugo de la Raza, given him eternity though his own internalization of his character's agony. But, now, *he*, Unamuno, needs to turn out more personal agony so that his own readers will now internalize *him*. It appears that the divine number seven (or seven times seven, maybe even seventy times seven) stands for the infinite number of continuations that may be necessary to achieve such a goal. Of course, if the narrative can be continued eternally, the cooperation of the reader will not be needed.

Two of the novellas included in the collection *San Manuel Bueno, mártir y tres historias más* have no epilogue, but *San Manuel Bueno, mártir* and *La novela de Don Sandalio* do. In the epilogue to *San Manuel Bueno, mártir*, the transcriber, "Unamuno," tells how the manuscript left by Ángela Carballino fell into his hands, and how he went about transforming it into the present document. With this explanation, the reader acknowledges that the text is not a biography but a novel, actually twice a novel, first, because it is the imaginative creation of Ángela, who, in her prologue paragraph, admitted "dreaming" her biography into being, and, second, because "Unamuno" is reconfiguring a dream that Ángela had previously textualized. Moreover, "Unamuno" winks at the reader, asking whether the type of narrative he is publishing reminds him or her of other narratives, such as *Niebla*, by this same "Unamuno." Finally he calls his narrative a "relato [...] novelesco" (2: 346) and states that a well-constructed fictional reality like that of Manuel Bueno is more phenomenically convincing than his own historical identity. This is undeniably true, for "Unamuno" himself is but a character and his duration in the reader has lasted only the time necessary to read the two pages of his epilogue.

The epilogue to *La novela de Don Sandalio* is much more complex. It must be recalled that, in the novella, an unnamed letter writer sends his friend Felipe a series of letters describing the actions of a chess player named Don Sandalio. Although the letter writer has several opportunities to learn intimate facts about the subject of his letters, he prefers to concentrate on the Don Sandalio that his own observations and inventiveness can create. In the epilogue, the prologuist-transcriber, an entity identfied in the epilogue as a well-known novelist (one might choose to call him "Unamuno") states his suspicion that the writer of the letters was really Don Sandalio, who has evoked the ruse of a third-person, extradiegetic narrator in order to achieve an illusion of objectivity. But no sooner does the epiloguist offer this theory than he switches to the more probable explanation that Felipe, the alleged narratee, has himself assembled the story. It really makes little difference whether Don Sandalio or Felipe has written the narrative, states "Unamuno" for, if Sandalio wrote it from another's imagined perspective, he is novelizing, and if Felipe wrote it as a biography, he is really basing the analysis of Sandalio's motivations on those that influence Felipe himself. Therefore, all biography is really autobiography, and all autobiography is a novel. The novelist who writes such a novel is, by the performance act of novelizing his own fantasies, creating the novel of his own life, and the writer who describes another's act of creating a novel is also novelizing himself by *performing* his description (carrying out the necessary thoughts and pen movements) for the possible creation of a text by still another party or narratee that the reader, in turn, will re-create in accord with his or her own dispositions and needs. "Unamuno" may or may not be the novelist describing Sandalio's or Felipe's creation of a novel, but at some place along the line he will have been one of the "readers," and therefore he will, for the time being, be the novelist mentally recreating the conveyed situation in accord with his own needs and abilities. Every reader is a "novelist," and every novelist by "novelizing" re-creates himself. *La novela de Don Sandalio* is a more clearly diagrammed and less writerly version of *Cómo se hace una novela*. Its epilogue is the entity that allows the reader to pull together all of the difficult but well-placed clues in the novella that "Don Sandalio," the "letter writer," the "unknown reader" of "Unamuno"'s previous novels, "Unamuno, " and the actual "reader" are continually and simultaneously performing these creative acts. All is a novel, and in a novel a new novelist with new possibilities—perhaps the ones that the reader needs—is bound to appear.

6
Epitexts

AN EPITEXT IS "ANY paratextual element not materially appended to the text but circulatiing [...] freely, in a virtually limitless physical and social space" (Genette 344). All of the articles, essays, letters, prologues, and creative works in which Unamuno refers, even obliquely and without naming them, to his narratives are obviously epitexts, and this means that—barring the development of an electronic concordance to the author's *Obras Completas* and correspondence, which would help in the identification of the most obvious epitexts—their actual number is virtually incalculable. These epitexts stand independent from the many, many thousands of intertexts that connect Unamuno's writings among themselves. An impressive example of the latter phenomenon—which is outside the scope of our purview—can be found in Tanganelli's recent volume *Unamuno fin de siglo: La escritura de la crisis*, in which important intertextual relationships are laid out for *Nuevo mundo* and its pre-texts, the *Diario íntimo* and its antecedents, the various compositional stages of the story "Beatriz" (1898), the play *La esfinge* (1898) and its drafts, the essay-meditation *Nicodemo el fariseo* (1899) and its six only recently published siblings once projected for the apocryphal *Meditaciones evangélicas*, and finally *Amor y pedagogía* (73-196).

In his edition of *Niebla*, Zubizarreta includes three of that narrative's many epitexts in a section titled "Textos complementarios," and we propose to use these as a very microcosmic illustration of the types of effects that an epitext can exercise on an Unamuno narrative. The epitexts in question are the articles "Tántalo," "Una entrevista con Augusto Pérez," and "Pirandello y yo," published repectively in *Los lunes de "El Imparcial"* (2 August 1909), *La Nación* of Buenos Aires (21 November, 1915), and *La Nación* of Buenos Aires (15 July, 1923). It will be apparent that the first of these saw light during the compositional phase of *Niebla*, the second right after publication, and the third nine years later. As Genette makes clear (345), there is often as much spread between the diachronic moments of the central narrative body as there is between the work's epitexts. The first of the articles collected by Zubizarreta discusses how Tantalus, in the version of Pindar, tried to steal the secret of immortality from the gods. It also speculates that Don Quijote, in the life beyond, held a conversation with Tantalus. We have here a mythologizing and a granting of universal significance to the struggle of Augusto Pérez to wrest immortality from "Unamuno" and God, coupled to a justification for creating new, posthumous episodes for the imaginable life beyond the grave of Unamuno's most famous character. (We have already discussed the way in which Augusto appears to "Unamuno" in a dream in the 1935 prologue to the third edition of *Niebla*.) "Una entrevista con Augusto Pérez" presents an imagined (dreamed) interview of Augusto supposedly carried out by "Unamuno" after the former's death. One interesting revelation of this interview is the way in which the resurrected character categorically states that "Unamuno" authorially killed him in *Niebla*, thus corroborating the version given in "Unamuno"'s post-prologue and denying Víctor's account of Augusto's willful suicide presented in the prologue. There is, however, a different side to this, for "when Augusto tells "Unamuno" to abandon the thought of reviving him, it is because he has come to realize that the basic reality of existence in time is its irreversable openness toward the future [...]" (Olson, *The Great Chiasmus* 98). That is, the "author" (who exists on the same diegetic plane as his character) may not be able to revive the character, but the co-creating reader standing outside the narrative may be able to do so at some future moment. Another intriguing perspective of the interview is

Augusto's association of the just-initiated Great War (World War I) with a frenetic nationalism that is, on the world stage, an "herostratic" equivalent to the desire for eternity that motivated Augusto. The most interesting lesson of the interview, however, is the reader's observation that Augusto appears to be decidedly more intelligent than his interviewer, "Unamuno," suggesting that, having completed his work, the "author" himself doubted his ability to wrestle a clear metaphysics from his 1914 narrative either during the creative process or at the moment of the interview. Only the character can explain what he underwent and may have learned. It is necessary to be within the hermeneutic circle to issue valid commentaries, and only the character and the reader who identifies with him have this privilege in Niebla. In the third of the epitexts collected by Zubizarreta, Unamuno takes up the similarity between the skeletal, metafictional dimensions of his *nivola* and the similar qualities that critics have noted in the plays of Luigi Pirandello, stating that, before the writing of Niebla, he knew nothing of Pirandello and is sure that Pirandello knew nothing of him.

Another important—perhaps the most important—epitext of Niebla is *Amor y pedagogía*. We call *Amor y pedagogía* an epitext because, despite its obvious, brief intertextuality with chapter 13 of Niebla, it silently functions as a paradigm that aids in reading the entirety of the latter work. Ribbans, as mentioned before, has carefully analyzed the many similarities between these two narratives that are connected by the encounter between Augusto Pérez and Avito Carrascal. Reading the two novels together—though Niebla in only an offhand way suggests we might do so—allows us to see how both works focus on what the character Entrambosmares, in chapter 13 of *Amor y pedagogía*, termed "herostratismo," the drive to eternalize one's name at all costs. (My own belief is that the chapter number 13—common to the herostratic exposition in both novels—is not pure coincidence.) In both works, "authors" try to create offspring that will live in the experiential memory of the reader. Avito tries to script a life for his son, to make him a genius that successive generations will admire and emulate. Víctor and

"Unamuno," on the other hand, heap suffering on Augusto so that the reader will internalize, not only the responses of their creation, but their own hidden existential conflicts that have been made the basis of Augusto's struggle for existence. Needless to say, a reading of *Amor y pedagogía* alerts the reader to the parallel importance of *Niebla*'s paratexts, while a reading of *Niebla* does the same for a reader of *Amor y pedagogía*. Both narratives prove, in Unamuno's hands, to be endlessly expandable, and the reader of one work easily perceives how the metaphysics and form of that work are immediately applicable to the form and metaphysics of the other. The fact that, years later, the epilogues to both *San Manuel Bueno, mártir* and *La novela de Don Sandalio* mention *Niebla* as the paragon of Unamuno narratives—a paragon with which the narratological techniques of *San Manuel* and *Don Sandalio* may be compared in an attempt to prove that "Unamuno" may be the author of both 1930s texts—gives added status to the 1914 narrative and urges the reader to let all three texts shed light on one another. Thus an epilogue, prologue, or note to one narrative may eventually become an epitext to others.

There are both public authorial expitexts and private authorial ones (Genette 345). An example of the first would be the published texts we have been discussing in the previous paragraphs. A private epitext would include diaries, letters, or comments made to friends. It is obvious that, in the case of a well-known figure, many private epitexts eventually become public. Most public authorial epitexts only indirectly comment on the central text, and many comments are so transparent that they go unperceived (346). One may, for example locate many allusions to both completed and planned narratives within the pages of *Del sentimiento trágico de la vida* without once finding an actual or proposed title. The same problem is even more frequent in private authorial epitexts. Unamuno repeatedly discussed his present and future work in thousands of letters to friends and other intellectuals, and it is only via the painful assembling of the references to the unnamed works mentioned in these letters that scholars have been able to piece together the way in which Unamuno's ideas and plots took form and the approximate dates on which important decisions were made. Zubizarreta's analysis of the structuring of *Cómo se hace una novela* and Robles's reconstruction of the stages in the composition of *Nuevo mundo* depend heavily on the collating of once private (but now public) epitexts. The same is true of the dating and reconstruction of the way in which Unamuno composed his *Diario íntimo* (published posthumously in 1970) and most of his poetry, especially that of *El Cristo de Velázquez* (1920) and the posthumous *Cancionero* (1953). Malvido Miguel's (245-273) tracing of the evolution of *Del sentimiento trágico de la vida* and Salcedo's (421-22) list of titles that Unamuno planned to use for his works come from similar epitexts.

Private authorial epitexts, such as letters, are written to a first addressee who is "interposed between the author and the possible public" (Genette 371). The author perceives this original addressee, not merely as an intermediary or pretext, but as a real individual, "even if the author's ulterior motive is to let the public subsequently stand witness to this interlocution" (371). Since Unamuno only rarely wrote any private text, including the *Diario íntimo* and the *Cancionero*, without envisioning its encounter with a reader beyond himself, it is difficult to believe that most of his letters were not also meant for posterity. His tendency to cite or paraphrase them (along with his addressees' answers) in paratexts would seem to be a backup technique for getting them into his public's hands, in case the literary scholarship of the future might fail. But who was this second intended addressee? It seems important to possess an answer, since Unamuno clearly would not write for X in the same way he would write for Y (Genette 371). Though, in practice, he was willing to send a letter to almost anyone that wrote him first, most of Unamuno's letters were intended for a public with the same love of words, willingness to grapple with an enthymeme or a chiasmus, and the same longing for immortality that he himself experienced. They are on the same high discursive level as the narratives themselves. Where their level is less elevated, they mesh well with the choppy, groping speech that Unamuno places in the mouths of his characters.

When the public reads private correspondence, it habitually makes allowances for the uncommon attributes that are associated with certain intended primary readers. A letter writer is often falsely modest when trying to please a publisher or established writer, hyperbolic about the difficulties of writing when approaching a writer or reader of his or her own literary class (373). The staged humility of the young Unamuno writing for a recommendation from already canonical writers like Galdós and Clarín is, at least today, almost comic. When, on the contrary, Unamuno wrote to his friends about the difficulty of composing *Nuevo mundo* and *Paz en la guerra*, he did not spare the details of his agony and, sometimes, his frustration in not having achieved somewhat more. *Abel Sánchez* appears like the product of an extremely clear mind, but Unamuno really suffered through the process of portraying Joaquín from the inside, as Milton had suffered with his Satan, and many letters show this angst. On the contrary, when Unamuno wrote to his editor Valentí Camp about his herculean efforts to expand *Amor y pedagogía* (Vauthier, "Epistolario" 433-520), he is extremely tight-lipped and compliant, because he is desperate to get a proto-*nivola* published after the failure of *Nuevo mundo* (Franz, "Nuevo mundo" 27-39).

One can appreciate the prologues and the epilogue to *Amor y pedagogía* more if one compares their unabashed satire of Valentí and the publisher Henrich to the inevitable frustration of what he was forced to keep under wraps in his letters to these same individuals. *Niebla*'s narrative planes, *La tía Tula*'s and *Tres novelas ejemplares*' brand of agonized spirituality, and all of the narratives' grounding in a hermeneutics that is uniquely Spanish can be better appreciated after reading Unamuno's correspondence with Clarín and Ganivet. It is mainly through the letters of Unamuno to his American translator, Warner Fite, that scholarship has been able to finally appreciate the self-interested use of sex on the part of Rosario in *Niebla* (Ribbans 122). The letters to Jiménez Ilundain add immeasurably to an appreciation of the ontological conflicts of Ignacio and Pachico in *Paz en la guerrra* and of Eugenio Rodero in *Nuevo mundo*. Letters to Pedro Mugica, Joan Maragall, and Luis Zulueta elucidate the fundamental strands of many narratives.

Later correspondence often discusses the critical reaction to earlier works (we also mentioned this in discussing prologues subsequent to the first), and in his reaction the author may distort what the critics have said in order to launch his own "contrary" opinions (Genette 380). To my mind, Unamuno does not distort the criticism he has received, this despite his frequent tendency to use his commentators as a foil. (Recall our comments about what Unamuno does with Cassou's "Retrato de Unamuno," written to accompany the first edition of *Cómo se hace una novela*.)

Diaries, too, are epitexts, and Unamuno produced many of them. The so-called *Diario íntimo* is the most famous, but there are also the collections of poems, *De Fuerteventura a París* and *Romancero del destierro* (1928), and finally the massive poetic *Cancionero*. Of these four, only the first and last can justly be termed personal epitexts, for the other two were soon sent off to the publisher. The *Diario íntimo* is intimately connected with the paradoxical problem of the public "persona" and the often contrary "real" personality explored with great intensity in most of the narratives beginning with *Niebla*. *De Fuerteventura a París* provides another variant of the autobiographical exile novelized in both the first version of *Cómo se hace una novela* and the bracketed additions to the second version. The composition of *Romancero del destierro* deals with the same material and conveniently overlaps the composition of both the 1926 and the 1927 editions of that narrative.

Pre-texts are epitextual manuscripts that their authors intentionally left behind. Pre-texts are deliberately made available posthumously "along with the degree of intention that attaches to such a gesture" but also without any guarantee of completeness (Genette 396). Few authors have left more pre-texts than Unamuno. Some, like the *Diario íntimo* and the *Cancionero* undoubtedly were intended for eventual publication. One can easily understand how Unamuno would feel unmasked if the thoughts of his 1897 religious crisis were made public in his lifetime. One can also comprehend that Unamuno might worry that the "mine of slag that might be worked patiently for nuggets of pure gold" (Nozick 190) that constitutes the *Cancionero* could lower his artistic standing, a situation that would be uncomfortable to endure during his lifetime. It is also undoubtably true that he did not expect to die on 31 December, 1936, when he was still adding poems to the collection. He was clearly planning new political and philosophical work of a different sort, and death surprised him without an opportunity to prepare the *Cancionero* for publication. Another very real possibility is that Unamuno considered the collection his *magnum opus*, an investment of eight long years and running the gamut from moments of spiritual transcendence to others of bitter atheism that might give the most complete picture possible of the soul of Miguel de Unamuno. Bequeathing such a "soul" to the public only after his death would make it complete and lend him the greatest possible chance of acquiring "eternity" in the poetic experience of his readers.

Other pre-texts are more problematic. When he died, Unamuno was working on a treatise provisionally titled *El resentimiento trágico de la vida*, whose notes have been scrupulously assembled and elucidated by Carlos Feal. Do thirty pages of undeveloped, highly ambiguous outline on the theme of envy constitute something the author wanted his public to see in its present form? One suspects not. We are given pause, however, by a recollection that, though *Del sentimiento trágico de la vida* and *La agonía del cristianismo* go over much of the same philosophical and religious ground using different source material, Unamuno insisted that his public have the 1925 work despite its rather more crude and unfinished nature. Just as he gave his reader *La agonía* as an eternal document of his exile, he might have been willing to yield the mere outline of *El resentimiento* as a testament to his agony during the first half year of the Civil War. Our suspicion that the work itself presents no new reasoning may be invalid for a writer like Unamuno, convinced—like Borges—that the same words in a new setting make for a radically different product.

Much more difficult is any judgment on the *Tratado del amor de Díos*, the partial forerunner of *Del sentimiento trágico de la vida* that Unamuno radically rewrote into a new work instead of publishing it in its initial form. A final judgment awaits the present work of Nelson Orringer and Paolo Tanganelli in, first, preparing critical editions and detailed commentaries for a public unable to read the manuscript preserved in the Unamuno Archives and, second, interpreting the significance of the work in Unamuno's evolution as a thinker and creative writer. Also awaiting eventual publication is the even earlier, positivistically charged—but in a highly unorthodox way (Ribas 107) *Filosofía lógica*—so well described by Zubizarreta (*Tras las huellas* 15-32) more than forty years ago. The latter manuscript has numerous epitexts of its own that comprise earlier attempts at the construction of a rational philosophic system (28-29). Tanganelli is also working with two additional unpublished essays that were worked into the *Tratado del amor de Dios*, one titled "Erostratismo" and another called "A la juventud española." At a recent conference, Tanganelli explained that study of all of these texts leads one to the conclusion that the emphasis on survival through fame that is paramount in "Erostratismo" and the *Tratado* does not receive the final emphasis in *Del sentimiento trágico de la vida* (Tanganelli, "Del erostratismo al *Amor de Dios*"). This detour from fame is, of course, not to be interpreted as a definitive pullback from the Unamunian endeavor to infuse his reader with the essence of his own personality, to "live" eternally within endless generations of readers, though vitally transformed by these readers into someone else, just as a continued terrestrial life would inevitably have transformed him. All of these texts appear to have been conserved by Unamuno—an indefatigable archivist of his every attempt at creation—so that his reader might inevitably come to know ever more of his life's infinite mutability, a mutability and vitality that he hopes to teach us is our own. Current work of Orringer on the *Tratado*, including its publication in both Spanish and English, is contributing and will soon contribute even more to our understanding of this vitality. Unamuno offered to send Ortega the manuscript of the *Tratado*, but Ortega discouraged him, objecting to its title and apparent lack of scientific rigor. Unamuno changed the title but became more convinced that his metaphysiscal purposes could be achieved only through an imaginative involvement of the reader (Orringer, "Del *Tratado*"). All of this doubtless has a great bearing on what Unamuno will try to achieve in the narratives he writes during and after the transformation of the *Tratado* into *Del sentimiento trágico de la vida*.

Vauthier ("Ironía," "El *Manual de quijotismo*") has recently brought to our attention two additional pre-texts, one existing in the archives of the Casa-Museo Unamuno in Salamanca, the other perhaps apocryphal. The first of these is a manuscript of some seventy folios titled *Manual de quijotismo*. The second, titled *Don Quijote en Fuerteventura*, is merely mentioned as a future project in the correspondence of Unamuno. Both the manuscript and the two titles (one perhaps merely evoking an idea *sans* plan for its development) are products of Unamuno's exile and appear to represent ideas concomitant to the writing of *Cómo se hace una novela*. In one work, Unamuno represents his exiled self as Don Quijote and the dictator Miguel Primo de Rivera as the vile Don Juan, while, in speaking of the other, he projects the intention of disgorging his own "drama íntimo" in order to create a work that is "éxtima." Both projected works are obviously, like *Cómo se hace una novela*, diary-narratives of Unamuno's exile, are ironic, even comic in tone, and appear to herald the comic vein that, with the notable exception of the brief observations of Zambrano (77), has seldom received serious exploration in studies of *Cómo se hace una novela*. We have here—as Vauthier makes clear—a new type of Unamunian humor, a synthesis of irony, sarcasm, indignation, and unrestrained cholera ("El *Manual de quijotismo*" 38-60; also *Arte de escribir* passim) designed to shake loose hope and action within the confines of Miguel Primo de Rivera's dictatorial Spain. It could not be any clearer that both planned works—one perhaps apocryphal, the other still unpublished except for brief extracts—evidence a deep involvement with Unamuno's metaphysics of play and Don Miguel's belief that the survival of both his fictional "author" and the real author is dependent on the reader's internalization and continued nurturing of the novelist's most vital conflicts.

Conclusions

ALTHOUGH UNAMUNO'S MAJOR NARRATIVES do not involve all of the paratextual forms labeled by Genette, they include most of them and, more often than not, these Unamunian paratexts produce twists and complexities that go far beyond the mere inventory of forms and corresponding effects carried out by the French theorist. Since Genette's evidence is based on a vast personal knowledge of Western narrative, one effect of our study of paratexts in Unamuno is a greatly expanded appreciation of the Basque author's complexity and creativity. One might be tempted to compare this inventiveness and control to a symphony in which the author creates expanding strands of relationship (narratological, metafictional, ontological) by demonstrating how epigraphs, prologues of different sorts, epilogues, notes, and epitexts transform one another into a multifaceted view of the origins, processes, and possible implications of the "narrative of life." Although his anti-Aristotelian, anti-Thomist convictions do not permit him to view these implications in a strictly metaphysical or ontological sense, the multifacted and ultimately open-ended nature of the relationships that his paratexts trace leads to a view that anything is possible in this narrative, including a fulfillment of the seemingly irrational but unerradicable desire to go on existing. I say that anything is possible in such a sea of paratexts in the same way that Foucault, in *The Order of Things* (3-16), detects an infinite posing of questions and potential answers in the juxtaposed creatures of Velázquz's *Las Meninas* and Culler, in his recent *Literary Theory: A Very Short Introduction*, posits theory's questioning of every convention of literary and humanistic study: "What is meaning? What is an author? What is it to read? What is the 'I' or subject who writes, reads, or acts?" (Cunningham 55).

This is not necessarily a comforting conclusion at which Unamuno's great essays—*Vida de Don Quijote y Sancho, Del sentimiento trágico de la vida, La agonía del cristianismo*—nor even the central narrative text of the novels clearly arrive. The former coalesce around a more problematic conviction that struggle and paradox—an *agon* between faith and reason, tragedy and irony, flesh and spirit—*may* lead to a personal or even communal conviction that the longing for eternity is a reflection of hidden realities denied by much empirical evidence. None of the essays skimp on a presentation of the negative factors. The key trope of the *Sentimiento trágico* is not the chiasmus, but the comparison or antithesis, introduced by the phrase "y sin embargo," which shows that, for every positive consideration, there is a corresponding negative (Franz, *The Word* 168ff). The central narrative text of the novels is no more encouraging, suggesting that Unamuno—in a way akin to that of later theorists like Benjamin, Bloom, de Man, and Derrida (Cunningham 61)—finds in both life and textualized living a type of "original brokenness." Eugenio Rodero perishes due to a disease that denies his conviction that human beings are not limited by the deadly "facts" adduced by reason. Ignacio dies a senseless death, having drowned his thoughts in a mist of tradition that ironically has brought him to a sad end. The despairing Apolodoro commits suicide. Augusto is either killed by "Unamuno" or takes his own life in rebellion against his limited freedom. Joaquín's only "eternal life" is a hope that his envy will last forever. Gertrudis unconvincingly repents of her crusade to endure through a manipulation of others. Raquel and Carolina resign themselves to the unhappy conclusion that the fullest life possible is one built on earthly power. The invincible Alejandro Gómez slits his veins upon realizing that his long-suffering wife is no longer at his side to assuage his mortality. Manuel Bueno, a partial Christ-figure, dies a reactionary and a liar, only to be beatified through a testimonial fraud. The letter writer in *Don Sandalio* is able to conserve his fantasies by a fearful refusal to look at the facts. Emeterio finds happiness in drowning his quest for meaning in wealth and earthly domesticity. Ricardo and Liduvina enter the monastic life, sublimating their failure to achieve transcendence through sexual rapture and the creation of life. There is doubtless an equivalent positive side to all of these narratives. The point is that, in the central text, Unamuno never obscures the grounds for a pessimistic response. The paratexts, however, by their open-ended dialogy with both each other and the attached central text, overwhelm the negative parts of the central text's dialectic. As in philosopher Nelson Goodman's exposition of the way in which artworks ultimately produce their own truth out of their inner language and the social milieu in which they necessarily receive interpretation, Unamuno's paratexts can be said to "create worlds that seem right in relation to our needs" (Freeland 168).

In order to arrive at such a perspective, it is, of course, necessary to move beyond a mere study of Unamuno's paratexts or of the paratexts coupled to a formalistic consideration of his novels as individualized wholes or as a group. One must also consider the paratextual forms and their imbedding in Unamunian novelistic structures in conjunction with the specific stylistic and dramatic messages of both his paratexts and his central text, messages that in Unamuno are always simultaneously metatextual and ontological. This is what this study has, from its very inception, attempted to do. It is obvious that no study of this nature is capable of bringing into play all of the possible structural, conceptual, poetic, and dramatic permutations of meaning inherent in Unamuno's novelistic texts and in the thousands of excellent critical studies that have accrued over the years. Even encyclopedic studies such as Cerezo's have unintentionally passed over important perspectives present in Unamuno's texts, in the precedents set by his philosophical and literary antecedents, and in many worthy studies that were not, at the moment of writing, sufficiently remembered to find their way into the product of critical exegesis. The author of the present study has had to be selective, using his experience to choose those details of the central narrative and those critical discoveries that seem to bear most on the functions of the paratexts. What has been amazing is to see how few studies have bothered to consider seriously and examine thoughtfully the presence of massive amounts of complex, paradoxically or (often) chiasmically arranged paratextual material. While a great deal of attention—sometimes concentrated but usually sparse—has been given to some particularities of the paratexts of *Amor y pedagogía*, *Niebla*, *Cómo se hace una novela*, *San Manuel Bueno, mártir* and *La novela de Don Sandalio*, practically none at all has been given to his other novels, and even those novels whose paratexts critics have favored continue to suffer for both lack of attention to the insights available in Genette's study and recognition of the piggybacking, ever-evolving, and self-innovating use of paratexts throughout Unamuno's novelistic career. This is all the more amazing, since the paratexts are literally "out there," separated from the central text, and seem therefore to be thrusting themselves into the view of the reader.

Unamuno favors prologues and epilogues. He is not beyond adding epilogues to prologues and epilogues alike. His epilogues do not correct his prologues but rather present an alternate perspective, most frequently a metatextual one that posits a "novelist" or "novelists" creating a text characterized by myriad voices and multiple perspectives. His second and third edition prologues affect the reading of the central text more than the initial prologues, because they are enriched with contradictory possibilities that occurred to Unamuno in hindsight over a long span of time. There is almost always an epistemological and metaphysical dimension to the prologues and epilogues that is attached to their metatexual preoccupations. Although, in his fiction, Unamuno does not favor epigraphs, he does sparingly use them and their effect is both ironic and metatextual. By placing his narrative into an intertextual relationship (sometimes an ironic one) with another book, he presents the perspective that the narrative being epigraphed is a literary artifact and is therefore open to whimsical or willful manipulation by both the author and the reader. As a professor of Greek, later Latin and historical linguistics, who uses his academic chairs to support his family while feeling little impulse to publish in his professional fields, Unamuno tends to use notes to narratives in order to parody pseudo-scientific discourse prior to privileging, for him and presumably also for us, a more inclusive literary one. He also employs notes to heighten the obvious: the fictional, inventive discourse of what he is annotating and the fact that such a discourse came to life in a particular historical and social setting which must be imagined in order to read the narrative in its original hermeneutics.

Since Unamuno was the author of an immense correspondence, important parts of which have been carefully collected, and since the Casa-Museo Unamuno in Salamanca retains some 30,000 letters on all matters that he received from writers, intellectuals, and common people alike, it stands to reason that these documents often shed light on his fiction. This light illumines the most probable dates on which Unamuno began to conceive or actually write particular narratives, the stages in a narratve's composition, ideas running through the novelist's mind during the period in which he wrote the work, editorial complications, changes of title, sources (both in life and in literature), and attitudes toward what he has accomplished or failed to do. The original editor of Unamuno's *Obras Completas*, Manuel García Blanco, set the standard for bringing correspondence to bear on the historical and emotional circumstances from which the novels allegedly sprang, but this unquestioned success unfortunately led to a great deal of misplaced emphasis upon retrieving the hidden intentionality of the narratives from the deliberate polyphony of the texts and the multiple real-life echoes that Unamuno narratively used. Many recent critics have successfully avoided this pitfall, but there are still many investigators who, anxious for a publication, scour archival material for "sources" that are as arbitrary as the preconceived, exegetic hunches of the *cervantófilo* that Unamuno parodies in the prologue he added to *Vida de Don Quijote y Sancho*.

Unfortunately, the distributional applicability of the correspondence is very uneven. While letters about the composition of most novels abound, there are presently almost none relating to what the present study consider's Unamuno's two most important narratives: *Niebla* and *Cómo se hace una novela*. The author was unusually secretive about the former, and the circumstances of exile and eventual neglect on the part of the French literary establishment did not permit him or encourage others to collect this correspondence during the years spent in France.

There are many additional epitextual sources: comments made in other Unamuno novels, in his articles and essays, in interviews with the press, in speeches and addresses, and in conversations with his family and friends. Most of this has been poorly collected and much must be assumed irreparably lost. The *Obras Completas* has compiled the texts of many of Unamuno's public orations from manuscripts made available to the press, but others are known only in summary form, such as they were reported in the newspapers. Interviews are always open to the distortion of the reporter or interlocutor, especially when hostile or recalling content from a distance of years. Recollections by members of Unamuno's immediate family, all now deceased, were usually idealized, heavy on circumstance but short on literature. Nevertheless, they usually accounted well for the author's use of time, monetary obsessions, conflicts with censorship, and domestic relationships that frequently found their way into his novels. It should be apparent from the matters discussed in this study that the prologue, epilogue, note, or appendix contained in one narrative often constitutes an epitext for another one, either because Unamuno explicitly discussed the earlier one in his more recent text, because one intuits that he is talking about a similar matter, or because he alludes to a project or work without naming it.

This study has ignored up to this point a few types of secondary paratexts that could profitably be explored in relation to Unamuno's narratives. Among these are the publisher, the place, and the date of publication. Robles (9-36) has traced Unamuno's unsuccessful attempts to locate friends who might think well of *Nuevo mundo* and eventually help him locate a publisher. The many letters collected and collated by this scholar show just how confident the author was about the merits of his narrative and how unanimous his friends were against recommending publication. Given the negative review that Azorín gave *Paz en la guerra* and the fact that Clarín tactfully refused to tell Unamuno what he thought of the narrative, it can only seem fortunate that he did not begin his career with a novel that, while anticipating splendidly the avant-garde form of *Amor y pedagogía*, had considerably less grasp of its story than either of the two novels that would begin to pave the way for Unamuno's role as a novelist. The fact that his long-time *contertulio* José Verdes Montenegro did not think well of Unamuno's attempt to publish the narrative about the anarchist Eugenio Rodero in *Las Noticias*, the socialist newspaper that Verdes edited in Bilbao (Robles 15), speaks volumes about the esthetic freedom that Unamuno was insisting upon after being chained for ten years to the communal spirit of *Paz en la guerra*. The Valentí Camp/Unamuno correspondence published and introduced by Vauthier (Introduction and notes 425-520) explains clearly the commercializing orientation of the Henrich publishing house and how that orientation forced drastic changes in the shape of *Amor y pedagogía*, a shape now redounding to Unamuno's credit owing to a remarkable sense of flexibility and play that is clearly visible in his letters to his editor. It may also be true that Henrich wanted Unamuno to place further stress on the remarkable metaliterary dimension of his narrative. We need to recall that in the same year that the publisher put out Unamuno's novel, it also published Azorín's *La Voluntad* and was reading and engineering changes in the manuscript of Baroja's *El mayorazgo de Labraz* (1903), two similarly metafictional novels (Rivas Hernández 65, 84). If Cassou's "Retrato de Unamuno" and lost contact with the original manuscript of *Cómo se hace una novela* were the sparks that ignited the writing of the masterful second version of this narrative, it can be said that the obstructionist letters from Valentí Camp were the spur that induced Unamuno to transform *Amor y pedagogía* into a narrative that today receives far more attention than during the first thirty years following its creation.

The attempt to publish *Nuevo mundo* in Bilbao evinces a writer of fiction still not ready to ply his trade in a larger world, this despite his recent successes in the essay form. The center of his narrative's action is a Madrid boarding house, but not the type of crossroads institution filled with bohemian types that Pérez de Ayala would soon excel at creating, but a small, dull place in which Rodero's attempts at the sexual conquest of his serving woman (a prelude to Augusto's shenanigans with Rosario in *Niebla*) are meant to use small-time transgressions as a vehicle for introducing metaphysical and metaliterary speculations for a minority that might care to read them. (It is clear from the letters marshaled by Robles that Unamuno's Bilbao correspondents did *not* care to bother with such dimensions). The subsequent publishing of *Paz en la guerra* and *Amor y pedagogía* in Madrid and Barcelona, on the other hand, shows a writer with more than enough vision and sufficient connections to gain exposure in a much wider and more competitive world. This admittedly is an impoverished and somewhat arbitrary collection of insights that one might—to offer an example—assemble from currently disseminated publishing data, but it is indicative of both what has to date been done and what one might conclude from or project to do with it.

One earnestly wishes that correspondence, bequeathed recollections, or interviews might be assembled to reconstruct the audience, the circumstance, and the publishing vehicle that Unamuno envisioned for all of his narratives. Why—other than the twenties' vogue of feminism, recently suggested by Johnson (160-70) was *La tía Tula*, begun before 1902, not published until 1921? Why did *Niebla*, largely written by 1907, not see completion until 1914? Why were the artistic successes *Niebla*, *Abel Sánchez*, and *La tía Tula* published to virtual perfection by Renacimiento but the compendia *Tres novelas ejemplares y un prólogo* and *San Manuel Bueno, mártir y tres historias más* put out by Espasa-Calpe, which succeeded in filling the latter volume with printing errors that Unamuno was forced to correct on his own author's copy? Was

Unamuno's ritual complaining about the payment that Renacimiento's director, Gregorio Martínez Sierra gave him the real factor, or was it that Unamuno learned of the latter's scandalous affair with and eventual remarriage to the actress Catalina Bárcena (O'Connor 39-41ff)? Or was Martínez Sierra's inability to appreciate Unamuno's philosophical and dramatic tensions—an inability that is transparent in the former's many letters to Don Miguel—the last straw? Or was it Martínez Sierra's long sojourns in South America and Hollywood that separated him from the day-to-day managment of his publishing interests the step that finally put an end to the relationship? Why was one of Unamuno's greatest narratives, *Tulio Montalbán y Julio Macedo* (originally published in the 11 December 1920 number of *La Novela Corta*), left out of these compendia while a number of inferior ones were included? Was it that Unamuno already preferred its dramatization, *Sombras de sueño* (1926) to the narrative, as the handwritten notes in his copy of the already published work might suggest, or was there some reason the work lost favor with him? (Unamuno always signed contracts guaranteeing his continued ownership of his work, a situation that discounts any notion that he was prevented from including the 1920 work in *Tres novelas ejemplares* or *Sam Manuel Bueno, mártir y tres historias más*.) What demands other than celebrity did the *Mercure de France* make on Unamuno prior to publishing the first (French) edition of *Cómo se hace una novela*? (Doubtless a French audience inspired, at least in part, the Parisian setting and the many intertexts with French literature, much as—according to Ouimette [10-60]—French issues exercised a great impact on the treatise *La agonía del cristianismo*.) The present author has not sought the prolonged access to archival material that would be necessary to begin in earnest the process of piecing together these puzzles, some of which have long frustrated scholars having daily contact with archives and *hemerotecas*. It is material that is most practically addressed by patient and unperterbable professors with year long sabbaticals, Spanish or other European scholars living near the possible sources, retired academics, or grantees able to convince the juries of granting agencies that such wide-ranging searches enjoy a high probability of success. In his scouring of Europe and America, in his labyrinthine following of leads, and in his willingness to purchase letters from the uninterested or financially conscious heirs of their recipients, Laureano Robles has done much toward initiating the solution of these puzzles.

Works Cited

Abellán, José Luis. *Miguel de Unamuno a la luz de la psicología: Una interpretación de Unamuno desde la psicología individual* Madrid: Tecnos, 1964.
Barrett, William. *The Illusion of Technique*. Garden City: Doubleday, 1978.
Blanco Aguinaga, Carlos. *El Unamuno contemplativo*. Mexico City: El Colegio de México, 1959.
Caballé, Ana. Introduction. *Amor y pedagogía*. By Miguel de Unamuno. 16th ed. Madrid: Espasa-Calpe, 1992. 9-35.
———. Introduction. *La tía Tula*. By Miguel de Unamuno. 18th ed. Madrid: Espasa-Calpe, 1990. 9-34.
Cerezo Galán, Pedro. *Las máscaras de lo trágico: Filosofía y tragedia en Miguel de Unamuno*. Madrid: Trotta, 1996.
Clavería, Carlos. *Temas de Unamuno*. 2nd ed. Madrid: Gredos, 1970.
Criado Miguel, Isabel. Introduction. *Abel Sánchez*. By Miguel de Unamuno. 9-44
———. *Las novelas de Miguel de Unamuno: Estudio formal y crítico*. Salamanca: Ediciones U de Salamanca, 1986.
Cunningham, Valentine. *Reading After Theory*. Oxford, England: Blackwell, 2002.
De Kock, Josse. *Introducción al Cancionero de Miguel de Unamuno* Madrid: Gredos, 1968.
Dewey, John. *Art as Experience*. New York: Perigee, 1980.
El tiempo de Miguel de Unamuno en Salamanca. Salamanca: Ediciones U de Salamanca, Excma. Diputación Provincial de Salamanca, Excmo. Ayuntamiento de Salamanca, 1998.
Feal Deibe, Carlos. *Unamuno, el otro y Don Juan*. Madrid: Cupsa, 1976.
Fish, Stanley. *Is There a Text in This Class? The Authority of Interpretive Communities*. Cambridge, MA: Harvard UP, 1980.
Foucault, Michel. *The Order of Things: An Archaeology of the Human Sciences*. N. trans. New York: Vintage, 1994.
Fox, Arturo A. *El Edipo en Unamuno y el espejo en Lacan*. Lewiston, NY: Edwin Mellen, 2001
Franz, Thomas R. "*Abel Sánchez* and Wilde's *The Picture of Dorian Gray*." *Letras Peninsulares*. 16.2 (2003). In press.

———. "Abel Sánchez y Le Colonel Chabert." *Revista Canadiense de Estudios Hispánicos* 24 (2000): 408-13.

———. "Agonía y auto(des)construcción en *Del sentimiento trágico de la vida.*" *Volumen homenaje cincuentenario de Miguel de Unamuno.* Ed. D. Gómez Molleda Salamanca: Casa-Museo Unamuno, 1986. 395-416.

———. *Niebla inexplorada: Midiendo intersticios en el maravilloso texto de Unamuno.* Newark, DE: Juan de la Cuesta, 2003.

———. "*Nuevo mundo* en la producción novelística unamuniana." *Cuadernos de la Cátedra Miguel de Unamuno* 33 (1998): 27-39.

———. "The Philosophical Bases of Fulgencio Entrambosmares in Unamuno's *Amor y pedagogía.*" *Hispania* 60 (1977): 443-51.

———. *The Word in the World: Unamuno's Tragic Sense of Language.* Athens, OH: Strathmore, 1987.

———. *Traces of the Muse: New Looks at the Spanish Novel from the Perspective of an Information Processing Age.* Athens, OH: Strathmore, 1991.

Freeland, Cynthia. *But is it Art? An Introduction to Art Theory.* Oxford, England: Oxford UP, 2001.

García Blanco, Manuel. Introduction. Vol. I of *Obras Completas* By Miguel de Unamuno. 7-58.

Genette, Gérard. *Paratexts: Thresholds of Interpretation.* Trans. Jane E. Lewin. Cambridge, England: Cambridge UP, 1997.

Gómez Blesa, Mercedes. Prologue. *Unamuno.* By María Zambrano. 9-25.

González López, Emilio. "La poesía de Unamuno: el relato poético *Teresa.*" *La Torre* 66 (1969): 84-89.

Gullón, Germán. Introduction. *Niebla.* By Miguel de Unamuno. 23rd ed. Madrid: Espasa-Calpe, 1990. 9-32.

———. "*Paz en la guerra* y la interiorización de la novela española moderna." *Ojáncano* 2 (1989): 41-57.

Gullón, Ricardo. *Autobiografías de Unamuno.* Madrid: Gredos, 1964.

———. *Técnicas de Galdós.* Madrid: Taurus, 1970.

James, William. *The Will to Believe and Others Essays in Popular Philosophy. Human Immortality.* New York: Dover, 1956.

Jameson, Frederic. *Postmodernism, or The Cultural Logic of Late Capitalism.* Durham: Duke UP, 1991.

Johnson Roberta. *Gender and Nation in the Spanish Modernist Novel.* Nashville: Vanderbilt UP, 2003.

Jurkevich, Gayana. *The Elusive Self: Archetypal Approaches to the Novels of Miguel de Unamuno*. Columbia: U of Missouri P, 1991.

———. "Unamuno's Anecdotal Digressions: Practical Joking and Narrative Structure in *Niebla*." *Revista Hispánic Moderna* 45 (1992): 3-14.

Kent, Conrad. *Luis González de la Huebra y los orígenes de la modernidad en Salamanca*. Salamanca: Junta de Castilla y León, 2001.

Kranzfelder, Ivo. *Edward Hopper, 1882-1967: Vision of Reality*. Trans. John William Gabriel. New York: Taschen, 1994.

La Rubia Prado, Francisco. *Alegorías de la voluntad: pensamiento, retórica y deconstrucción en la obra de Miguel de Unamuno*. Madrid: Libertarias/Prodhufi, 1996.

La Santa Biblia. Madrid: Ediciones Paulinas, 1972.

López-Marrón, José. *Unamuno y su camino a la individualización*. New York: Peter Lang, 1998.

Maíz, Claudio. *De París a Salamanca: Trayectorias de la modernidad en Hispanoamérica. Aportes para el estudio del novecentismo*. Salamanca: Ediciones Universidad de Salamanca, 2004.

Malvido Miguel, Eduardo. *Unamuno a la busca de la inmortalidad (Estudio* Del Sentimiento trágico de la vida*)*. Salamanca: Ediciones San Pío X, 1977.

Marías, Julián. *Miguel de Unamuno*. 3rd ed. Madrid: Espasa-Calpe, 1997.

Marichal, Juan. "La originalidad de Unamuno en la literatura de confesión." *El designio de Unamuno*. Madrid: Taurus, 2002. 49-78.

Mermall, Thomas. "The Chiasmus: Unamuno's Master Trope." *PMLA* 105 (1990): 245-55.

———. *La retórica del humanismo: La cultura española después de Ortega*. Madrid: Taurus, 1978.

Mezquita, Eduardo Pascual. *La política del último Unamuno*. Salamanca: Globalia Ediciones Anthema, 2003.

Miller, Stephen. "Reading Galdós Illustrated: The Riddle of the Sphinx in *La corte de Carlos IV*." *Romance Quarterly* 52 (2005): 101-07.

Nozick, Martin. *Miguel de Unamuno: The Agony of Belief*. Princeton: Princeton UP, 1982

O'Connor, Patricia. *Mito y realidad de una dramaturgia española: María Martínez Sierra*. Logroño: Gobierno de La Rioja/ Instituto de Estudios Riojanos, 2003

Olson, Paul R. "Sobre las estructuras quiásticas en el pensamiento unamuniano (interpretación de un juego de palabras)." In *Homenaje a Juan López Morillas*. Ed. José Amor y Vásquez And David A, Kossof. Madrid: Castalia,1982. 359-68

———. *The Great Chiasmus: Word and Flesh in the Novels of Unamuno*. West Lafayette: Purdue UP, 2003.

Orringer, Nelson. "Del *Tratado del amor de Dios* a *Del sentimiento trágico*: historia de un ensayo de universalidad." V Jornadas Unamunianas. University of Salamanca, Spain. 24 October 2003.

Ouimette, Victor. Introduction. *La agonía del cristianismo*. By Miguel de Unamuno. Madrid: Espasa-Calpe, 1996. 9-62.

Øveraas, Anne Marie. *Niebla contra nivola*. Salamanca: Ediciones U de Salamanca, 1993.

Pérez, Janet. "Rhetorical Integration in Unamuno's *Niebla*." *Revista Canadiense de Estudios Hispánicos* 8 (1983): 49-73.

Pérez López, Manuel María. "Unamuno: estrategias expresivas del relativismo." *Cuadernos de la Cátedra Miguel de Unamuno*, 38 (2003): 63-89.

Porqueras Mayo, Arturo. *El prólogo como género literario. Su estudio en el Siglo de Oro español*. Madrid: Consejo Superior de Investigaciones Científicas, 1957.

Ribas, Pedro. *Para leer a Unamuno*. Madrid: Alianza, 2002.

Ribbans, Geoffrey. *Niebla y soledad: aspectos de Unamuno y Machado*. Madrid: Gredos, 1971

Rivas Hernández, Ascensión. *Pío Baroja: aspectos de la técnica narrativa*. Cáceres: U de Extremadura, 1998.

Robles, Laurano. Introduction. *Nuevo mundo*. By Miguel de Unamuno. 9-39.

Salcedo, Emilio. *Vida de don Miguel*. Salamanca: Anaya, 1964.

Sánchez Barbudo, Antonio. *Estudios sobre Unamuno y Machado*. Madrid: Guadarrama, 1959.

Schenk, H.G. *The Mind of the European Romantics*. Garden City: Doubleday, 1969.

Sinclair, Alison. *Uncovering the Mind: Unamuno, the Unknown and the Vicissitudes of Self*. Manchester, England: Manchester UP, 2001.

Spires, Robert C. *Transparent Simulacra: Spanish Fiction, 1902-1826*. Columbia: U of Missouri P, 1988.

Tanganelli, Paolo. "Del erostratismo al *Amor de Dios*." V Jornadas Unamunianas. Salamanca, Spain. 24 October. 2003.

———. *Hermenéutica de la crisis en la obra de Unamuno entre finales del XIX y comienzos del XX: La "crisis del 97" como posible exemplum de la crisis finisecular*. Salamanca: U de Salamanca, 2001.

———. "Introduzzione. *Nuevo mundo*: tra modernismo letterario e fabulazione romántica." *Nuovo mondo*. De Miguel de Unamuno. Ed. Paolo Tanganelli. Trad. Sandro Borzoni. Caserta: Edizioni Saletta dell'Uva, 2005. 7-27.

———. *Unamuno fin de siglo: La escritura de la crisis*. Pisa: Edzioni ETS, 2003.
Ulmer, Gregory. *The Legend of Herostratus: Existential Envy in Rousseau and Unamuno*. Gainesville: UP of Florida, 1977.
Unamuno, Miguel de. *Abel Sánchez*. Ed. Isabel Criado 19th ed. Madrid: Espasa-Calpe, 1990.
———. *Amor y pedagogía*. Barcelona: Henrich, 1902
———. *Cómo se hace una novela*. Buenos Aires: Alba, 1927.
———. *El resentimiento trágico de la vida: Notas sobre la revolución y guerra civil españolas*. Ed. Carlos Feal. Madrid: Alianza, 1991.
———. *Manual de quijotismo; Cómo se hace una novela; Epistolario Miguel de Unamuno/Jean Cassou*. Ed. Bénédicte Vauthier Salamanca: Ediciones U de Salamanca, 2005.
———. *La tía Tula*. Madrid: Renacimiento, 1921.
———. *Nuevo mundo*. Ed. Laureano Robles. Madrid: Trotta, 1994.
———. *Niebla*. Madrid: Renacimiento, 1914.
———. *Obras Completas*. Ed. Manuel García Blanco. 9 vols. Madrid: Escelicer, 1966-1971.
———. *Obras Completas*. Ed. Ricardo Senabre. 5 vols. Madrid: Turner 1995-2003.
———. *Paz en la guerra*. Madrid: Fernando Fe, 1897.
———. *Poesía Completa*. Ed. Ana Suárez Miramón. 4 vols. Madrid: Alianza, 1987-1989.
———. *San Manuel Bueno, Mártir*. *La Novela de Hoy*. 10.36 (1931). Fills the entire number.
———. *San Manuel Bueno, mártir y tres historias más*, Madrid: Espasa-Calpe, 1933.
———. *Tulio Montalbán y Julio Macedo*. *La Novela Corta*. 5.260 (1920). Fills the entire number.
Unamuno Pérez, María de la Concepción. *Miguel de Unamuno y la cultura francesa*. Salamanca: Ediciones U de Salamanca, 1991.
Valdés, Mario. Introduction. *San Manuel Bueno, mártir*. By Miguel de Unamuno. Madrid: Cátedra, 1979. 13-81.
Vauthier, Bénédicte. *Arte de escribir e ironía en la obra narrativa de Miguel de Unamuno*. Salamanca: Ediciones U de Salamanca, 2004.
———. "El *Manual de quijotismo* y *Cómo se hace una novela*: diário éxtimo y cuaderno de bitácora de una novela sin escribir." *Cuadernos de la Cátedra Miguel de Unamuno* 36 (2001): 13-60. Also in introduction to Miguel de Unamuno, *Manual de quijotismo; Cómo se hace una novela; Epistolario Miguel de Unamuno/Jean Cassou*. 13-61.

———. Introduction and notes. "Epistolario Unamuno/ Santiago Valentí Camp." *Amor y pedagogía*. By Miguel de Unamuno. Madrid: Biblioteca Nueva, 2002. 13-129, 433-520.

———. "Ironía, censura y retórica de la cólera en el diario éxtimo del exilio." *Miguel de Unamuno: Estudios sobre su obra II: Actas de las V Jornadas Unamunianas, Salamanca, Casa-Museo Unamuno, 23 a 25 de octubre de 2003*. Salamanca: Ediciones U de Salamanca, 2003. 113-27. Also as introduction in Miguel de Unamuno. *Manual de quijotismo; Cómo se hace una novela; Epistolario Miguel de Unamuno/Jean Cassou*. 13-61.

———. *Niebla de Miguel de Unamuno: A favor de Cervantes, en contra de los "cervantófilos." Estudio de narratología estiliística*. Bern: Peter Lang, 1999.

Zambrano, María. *Unamuno*. Ed. Mercedes Gómez Blesa. Barcelona: Debate, 2003.

Zubizarreta, Armando F. Introduction and notes. *Niebla*. By Miguel de Unamuno. Madrid: Castalia, 1995. 7-61.

———. *Tras las huellas de Unamuno*. Madrid: Taurus, 1960.

———. *Unamuno en su nivola*. Madrid: Taurus, 1960.

Zubiri, Xavier. *Estructura dinámica de la realidad*. Madrid: Alianza/ Fundación Xavier Zubiri, 1989.

Printed in the United States
45655LVS00007B/199-246